Wesleyan Methodist Church in Canada

The Doctrines and Discipline of the Wesleyan Methodist Church in Canada

Wesleyan Methodist Church in Canada

The Doctrines and Discipline of the Wesleyan Methodist Church in Canada

ISBN/EAN: 9783337189693

Printed in Europe, USA, Canada, Australia, Japan

Cover: Foto ©Lupo / pixelio.de

More available books at **www.hansebooks.com**

THE

DOCTRINES AND DISCIPLINE

OF THE

WESLEYAN METHODIST CHURCH

IN CANADA.

Published by Order of the Conference.

TORONTO:
SAMUEL ROSE, WESLEYAN BOOK-ROOM,
KING STREET EAST.

1870.

CONTENTS.

CHAPTER I.

	Page
Sec. 1. Articles of Religion	1

CHAPTER II.

Church Courts.

Sec. 1. Of the Conference	9
2. Of District Meetings	15
3. Of Local Preachers and their Meetings	29
4. Of Quarterly Official Meetings	32

CHAPTER III.

Ministers, Preachers, and their Duties.

Sec. 1. Of the Appointment of Presidents and their Duties	34
2. Of Chairmen of Districts and their Duties	36
3. Of the Duties of Superintendents	38
4. Of the Duty of Travelling Preachers	43
5. Of the Election and Ordination of Ministers, and their Duties	45
6. Of the Reception of Ministers from other Churches	46
7. Of the Rules by which we should Continue or Desist from Preaching at any place	47
8. Of the Matter and Manner of Preaching, and of other Public Exercises	48

		Page
Sec. 9.	Of the Duties of Ministers and Preachers to God, themselves, and one another	49
10.	Of Visiting from House to House, and enforcing Practical religion	51
11.	Of Employing our Time Profitably, when not engaged in Public Exercises	56
12.	Of the Necessity of Union among Ourselves	57
13.	Of the Relation of Baptized Children to the Church	58
14.	Of Public Worship	60
15.	Of the Sacraments	61
16.	Of the Spirit and Truth of Singing	62

CHAPTER IV.
Of Members of the Church.

Sec. 1.	Of the Origin, Design, and General Rules of our United Societies	63
2.	Of the Band Societies	67
3.	Of Class Meetings	70
4.	Of Marriage	72
5.	Of Dress	73

CHAPTER V.
Of bringing Ministers and Members to Trial, and of Insolvencies and the Settlement of Disputes.

Sec. 1.	Of the Trial of Ministers and Travelling Preachers	74
2.	Of the Trial of Local Preachers	77
3.	Of the Trial of Members of the Church	79

CHAPTER VI.
Temporal Economy.

Sec 1.	Of the Boundaries of the Conference, &c	83
2.	Of the Salaries of Ministers and Preachers, and the Allowances to their Wives, Widows, and Children	84

CONTENTS. v

	Page
Sec. 3. Of the Qualifications, Appointment, and Duties of the Stewards of Circuits	86
4. Of the Building of Churches and Parsonages, and the order to be observed therein	88

Chapter VII.
Sacramental and other Services.

Sec. 1. Of the Ministration of Baptism to Infants	92
2. Of the Ministration of Baptism to Adults	95
3. Of the Lord's Supper	99
4. Of the Form and Manner of Ordaining Ministers	107
5. Of the Form of Solemnization of Matrimony	116
6. Of the Order of the Burial of the Dead	121
7. Of the Form of Renewing the Covenant	124
8. Of the Form for Laying the Corner-Stone of a Church	139
9. Of the Form for the Dedication of a Church	145

Chapter VIII.
On the Constitution of the Funds and Committees of Connexional Societies.

Sec. 1. Of the Book and Printing Establishment	151
2. Of the Superannuated Ministers' Fund	154
3. Of the Contingent Fund	156
4. Of the Children's Fund	158
5. Of the Church Relief Fund	162
6. Of the Educational Fund	164
7. Of the Revised Constitution of the Missionary Society of the W. M. Church in Canada	165

Chapter IX.

Articles of Union between the British Wesleyan Methodist Conference and the Conference of the Wesleyan Methodist Church in Canada	169
Model Deed	177

DOCTRINES AND DISCIPLINE.

CHAPTER I.

ARTICLES OF RELIGION.

I. *Of Faith in the Holy Trinity.*

THERE is but one living and true God, everlasting, without body or parts, of infinite power, wisdom, and goodness; the maker and preserver of all things, visible and invisible. And in unity of this Godhead there are three Persons, of one substance, power, and eternity: the Father, the Son, and the Holy Ghost.

II. *Of the Word, or Son of God, who was made very man.*

The Son, who is the Word of the Father, the very and Eternal God, of one substance with the Father, took man's nature in the womb of the blessed Virgin; so that two whole and perfect natures, that is to say, the Godhead and Manhood, were joined together in one person, never to be divided, whereof is one Christ, very God and very man, who truly suffered, was crucified, dead, and buried, to reconcile his Father to us, and to be a sacrifice, not only for original guilt, but also for the actual sins of men.

III. *Of the Resurrection of Christ.*

Christ did truly rise again from the dead, and took again his body, with all things appertaining to the perfection of man's nature, wherewith he ascended into Heaven, and there sitteth until he returns to judge all men at the last day.

IV. *Of the Holy Ghost.*

The Holy Ghost, proceeding from the Father and the Son, is of one substance, majesty, and glory with the Father and the Son, very and eternal God.

V. *The Sufficiency of the Holy Scriptures for Salvation.*

The Holy Scriptures contain all things necessary to salvation; so that whatsoever is not read therein, nor may be proved thereby, is not to be required of any man that it should be believed as an article of faith, or be thought requisite or necessary to salvation. In the name of the Holy Scriptures, we do understand those canonical books of the Old and new Testament, of whose authority was never any doubt in the Church.

THE NAMES OF THE CANONICAL BOOKS.

Genesis.	The First Book of Chronicles.
Exodus.	The Second Book of Chronicles.
Leviticus.	The Book of Ezra.
Numbers.	The Book of Nehemiah.
Deuteronomy.	The Book of Esther.
Joshua.	The Book of Job.
Judges.	The Psalms.
Ruth.	The Proverbs.
The First Book of Samuel.	Ecclesiastes, or the Preacher.
The Second Book of Samuel.	Canticles, or Songs of Solomon.
The First Book of Kings.	Four Prophets the greater.
The Second Book of Kings.	Twelve Prophets the less.

All the Books of the New Testament, as they are commonly received, we do receive and account canonical.

VI. *Of the Old Testament.*

The Old Testament is not contrary to the New; for both in the Old and New Testament everlasting life is offered to mankind by Christ, who is the only Mediator between God and man. Wherefore they are not to be heard, who feign that the old fathers did look only for transitory promises. Although the law given from God to Moses, as touching ceremonies and rites, doth not bind Christians, nor ought the civil precepts thereof of necessity to be received in any commonwealth; yet notwithstanding, no Christian whatsoever is free from the obedience of the commandments which are called moral.

VII. *Of Original or Birth Sin.*

Original sin standeth not in the following of Adam, (as the Pelagians do vainly talk), but it is the corruption of the nature of every man that naturally is engendered of the offspring of Adam, whereby man is very far gone from original righteousness, and of his own nature inclined to evil, and that continually.

VIII. *Of Free Will.*

The condition of man after the fall of Adam is such that he cannot turn and prepare himself by his own natural strength and works, to faith, and calling upon God; wherefore we have no power to do good works, pleasant and acceptable to God, without the grace of God by Christ preventing us, that we may have a good will, and working with us when we have that good will.

IX. *Of the Justification of Man.*

We are accounted righteous before God, only for the merit of our Lord and Saviour Jesus Christ, by faith, and not for our own works or deservings: Wherefore, that we are justified by faith only, is a most wholesome doctrine and very full of comfort.

X. *Of Good Works.*

Although good works, which are the fruits of faith, and follow after justification, cannot put away our sins, and endure the severity of God's judgment, yet are they pleasing and acceptable to God in Christ, and spring out of a true and lively faith, insomuch that by them a lively faith may be as evidently known as a tree is discerned by its fruit.

XI. *Of Works of Supererogation.*

Voluntary works, besides, over and above God's commandments, which are called works of supererogation, cannot be taught without arrogance and impiety. For by them men do declare that they do not only render unto God as much as they are bound to do, but that they do more for his sake than that of bounden duty is required; Whereas Christ saith plainly, When ye have done all that is commanded you, say, We are unprofitable servants.

XII. *Of Sin after Justification.*

Not every sin willingly committed after justification is the sin against the Holy Ghost, and unpardonable. Wherefore, the grant of repentance is not to be denied to such as fall into sin after justification: After we have received the Holy Ghost, we may depart from grace given, and fall into sin, and by the grace of God rise again and amend our lives. And therefore they are to be condemned who say they can no more sin as long as they live here, or deny the place of forgiveness to such as truly repent.

XIII. *Of the Church.*

The visible Church of Christ is a congregation of faithful men, in which the pure word of God is preached, and the sacraments duly administered according to Christ's ordinance, in all those things that of necessity are requisite to the same.

XIV. *Of Purgatory.*

The Romish doctrine concerning purgatory, pardon, worshipping, and adoration, as well of images as of relics, and also invocation of saints, is a fond thing, vainly invented, and grounded upon no warrant of Scripture, but repugnant to the word of God.

XV. *Of Speaking in the Congregation in such a Tongue as the People understand not.*

It is a thing plainly repugnant to the Word of God, and the custom of the Primitive Church, to have public prayer in the church, or to minister the Sacraments, in a tongue not understood by the people.

XVI. *Of the Sacraments.*

Sacraments ordained of Christ are not only badges or tokens of Christian men's profession, but rather they are certain signs of grace, and God's good-will towards us, by the which he doth work invisibly in us, and doth not only quicken, but also strengthen and comfort our faith in him.

There are two Sacraments, ordained of Christ our Lord in the Gospel; that is to say, Baptism and the Supper of the Lord.

Those five commonly called Sacraments,—that is to say, Confirmation, Penance, Orders, Matrimony, and Extreme Unction,—are not to be counted for Sacraments of the

Gospel, being such as have partly grown out of the *corrupt* following of the Apostles; and partly are states of life allowed in the Scripture, but yet have not the like nature of Baptism and the Lord's Supper, because they have not any visible sign or ceremony ordained of God.

The Sacraments were not ordained of Christ to be gazed upon, or to be carried about; but that we should duly use them. And in such only as worthily receive the same they have a wholesome effect or operation; but they that receive them unworthily, purchase to themselves condemnation, as Saint Paul saith, 1 Cor. xi. 29.

XVII. *Of Baptism.*

Baptism is not only a sign of profession and mark of difference, whereby Christians are distinguished from others that are not baptised, but it is also a sign of regeneration, or the new birth. The baptism of young children is to be retained in the church.

XVIII. *Of the Lord's Supper.*

The Supper of the Lord is not only a sign that Christians ought to have among themselves one to another, but rather is a Sacrament of our redemption by Christ's death; insomuch that to such as rightly, worthily, and with faith receive the same, the bread which we break is a partaking of the body of Christ, and likewise the cup of blessing is a partaking of the blood of Christ.

Transubstantiation, or the change of the substance of bread and wine in the Supper of our Lord, cannot be proved by Holy Writ, but is repugnant to the plain words of Scripture, overthroweth the nature of a Sacrament, and hath given occasion to many superstitions.

The body of Christ is given, taken, and eaten, in the Supper, only after a heavenly and spiritual manner. And the means whereby the body of Christ is received and eaten in the Supper, is faith.

The Sacrament of the Lord's Supper was not by Christ's ordinance reserved, carried about, lifted up, or worshipped.

XIX. *Of both Kinds.*

The cup of the Lord is not to be denied to the lay-people, for both the parts of the Lord's Supper, by Christ's ordinance and commandment, ought to be administered to all Christians alike.

XX. *Of the one Oblation of Christ, finished upon the Cross.*

The offering of Christ once made, is that perfect redemption, propitiation, and satisfaction for all the sins of the whole world, both original and actual: and there is none other satisfaction for sin but that alone. Wherefore the sacrifice of mass, in which it is commonly said that the priest doth offer Christ for the quick and the dead, to have remission of pain or guilt, is a blasphemous fable and dangerous deceit.

XXI. *Of the Marriage of Ministers.*

The ministers of Christ are not commanded by God's law either to vow the estate of single life or to abstain from marriage; therefore it is lawful for them, as for all other Christians, to marry at their own discretion, as they shall judge the same to serve best to godliness.

XXII. *Of the Rites and Ceremonies of the Church.*

It is not necessary that rites and ceremonies should in all places be the same, or exactly alike; for they have been always different, and may be changed according to the diversity of countries, times, and men's manners, so that nothing be ordained against God's word. Whosoever, through his private judgment, willingly and purposely doth openly break the rites and ceremonies of the church to which he belongs, which are not repugnant to the word of God, and are ordained and approved by common authority, ought to be rebuked openly, that others may fear to do the like, as one that offendeth against the common order of the church, and woundeth the consciences of weak brethren.

Every particular church may ordain, change, or abolish rites and ceremonies, so that all things may be done to edification.

XXIII. *Of the Civil Government.*

We believe it is the duty of all Christians to be subject to the powers that be; for we are commanded by the Word of God to respect and obey the Civil Government. We should therefore not only fear God, but honour the King.

XXIV. *Of Christian Men's Goods.*

The riches and goods of Christians are not common as touching the right, title, and possession of the same, as some do falsely boast. Nothwithstanding, every man ought, of such things as he possesseth, liberally to give alms to the poor, according to his ability.

XXV. *Of a Christian Man's Oath.*

As we confess that vain and rash swearing is forbidden Christian men by our Lord Jesus Christ, and James, his Apostle, so we judge that the Christian religion doth not prohibit but that a man may swear when the magistrate requireth, in the cause of faith and charity, so it be according to the Prophet's teaching, in justice, judgment, and truth.

CHAPTER II.

CHURCH COURTS.

SECTION I.

OF THE CONFERENCE.

It is desired that all things be considered on these occasions as in the immediate presence of God; that every person speak freely whatever is in his heart.

Ques. 1. How may we best improve our time at the Conference?

Ans. 1. While we are conversing, let us have an especial care to set God always before us.

2. In the intermediate hours let us redeem all the time we can for private exercises.

3. Therein let us give ourselves to prayer for one another, and for a blessing on our labour.

Ques. 2. Who shall compose the Conference, and what are the regulations and powers belonging to it?

Ans. 1. The Conference, in its extended sense, is constituted as defined in the Model Deed.

2. The Conference, assembled for the transaction of business, shall be composed of the President, Ex-President, and other Conference officers, and all Ministers who have been appointed by their District Meetings to attend; whose duty it shall be to remain till the close of the Conference: Nevertheless, other Ministers in full connection, who may be present, may take part in the proceedings as members.

The Conference shall have authority to locate any of its members by a majority of three-fourths, provided no person shall be located without one year's notice, or after he has travelled fifteen years; and the Conference shall afford such assistance to any brother so retiring as it may be able and judge expedient.

3. At all times, when the Conference is met, it shall take a majority of those appointed by the District Meetings to attend to constitute a quorum for transacting business.

4. The Conference shall have full power to make rules and regulations for the Church, under the following limitations and restrictions, viz :—

First.—The Conference shall not make, alter, or change our Articles of Religion, nor establish any new standards of doctrine, contrary to our present existing and established standards of doctrine.

Second.—They shall not change or alter, or make any regulations that will interfere with, or infringe the Articles of Union between this and the British Conference, ratified in the year 1847.

Third.—They shall not revoke or change the General Rules of the United Societies.

Fourth.—They shall not do away with the privileges of our Ministers or Preachers of trial by a committee, and of an appeal; neither shall they do away with the privileges of our Members of trial before the society, or by a committee, and of an appeal.

Fifth.—They shall not appropriate the profits of the Book Room to any purpose other than for the benefit of the travelling Ministers and Preachers, the Superannuated Ministers, their widows and children.

Sixth.—No new rule or regulation, or alteration of any

rule or regulation now in force, respecting our temporal economy, such as the building of churches, the order to be observed therein; the allowance to the Ministers and Preachers, their widows and children; the raising annual supplies for the propagation of the Gospel (the Missions excepted); for making up the allowances of the Ministers, Preachers, &c.; shall be considered as of any force or authority, till such rule, regulation, or alteration shall have been laid before the several Quarterly Official Meetings throughout the whole Connexion, and shall have received the consent of a majority of the members, who may be present at the time of laying such rule, regulation or alteration before them, of two-thirds of the said Quarterly Official Meetings.

Seventh.—Nor shall any new rule, regulation or alteration, respecting the doctrines of our Church, the rights and privileges of our members, such as the receiving persons on trial, and into full connexion, the conditions on which they shall retain their membership, the manner of bringing to trial, finding guilty, and reproving, suspending, or excluding disorderly persons from Church privileges, have any force or authority until laid before the Quarterly Official Meetings, and approved as aforesaid: Provided, nevertheless, that a vote of a majority of two-thirds of the Ministers appointed to attend the Conference shall suffice to alter or do away any of the above restrictions, except the first, sixth, and seventh, which shall not be done away or altered without the consent of two-thirds of the Quarterly Official Meetings throughout the Connexion; also, except the second restriction, which shall not be done away or altered without the recommendation or consent of the British Conference.

Any resolution involving a change in the principles and rules of our economy shall require for its adoption a majority of two-thirds of the Conference.

Ques. 3. Who shall appoint the time and place of holding the sessions of the Conference?

Ans. The Conference shall appoint the time and place of its own sitting.

Ques. 4. What is the usual order of conducting the business of the Conference?

Ans. After the President has opened the Conference with the usual devotional exercises, he shall inquire,—

1. Who have been appointed by the respective District Meetings to attend the Conference; and what members of Conference are now present?

After which the Secretary shall be elected by ballot.

2. Are there any objections to any of our Ministers or Preachers?

3. Who compose the several Conference Committees?—
—The Stationing Committee?—Pastoral Address?—Reply to British Conference Address?—On Memorials and Miscellaneous Resolutions?—On Revision and Returns?—Sabbath Schools?—Contingent Fund?—Children's Fund?—Church Relief Fund?—Education of Candidates for our Ministry?—And the Missionary Committee?—and, What Laymen are appointed for the several Committees on Connexional Funds?

4. What Preachers are this year admitted into full connection with the Conference and ordained?

5. What Preachers remain on *trial?*
   Who have travelled *three* years?
   Who have travelled *two* years?
   Who have travelled *one* year?

6. What Preachers are on the List of Reserve?

7. What Preachers are now received on trial?

8. Who have died since last Conference?

THE CONFERENCE. 13

9. Who are the Superannuated Ministers?

10. Who are the Supernumerary Ministers?

12. What persons, who were in full connection with the Conference, *now cease to be recognized* as Ministers among us?

12. Who are now deposed from the office of the Ministry?

13. Who are now deposed from the office of the Ministry, and expelled from the Church?

14. How are the Ministers and Preachers stationed for the ensuing year?

15. What is the number of Church Members, Places of Worship, Attendance on Worship, on each Circuit and Mission? What is the number of Baptisms administered, and Marriages solemnized by each Minister?

16. What is the number of Ministers, Preachers, and Laymen, in the Quarterly official Meetings? Of Sabbath Schools? and, What Connexional Property? These questions to be answered in accordance with the authorized Conference Schedule.

17. What has been collected on each District for the various Connexional Funds? Have these amounts been remitted at the proper time to the several Treasurers; and paid over to the several claimants?

18. What are the Reports of the several Committees?— The Book Committee? Pastoral Address? Reply to British Conference Address? On Memorials and Miscellaneous Resolutions? On Revision and Returns? Sabbath Schools? Contingent Fund? Children's Fund? Church Relief Fund? Education of Candidates for our Ministry? Superannuation Fund?

19. What further measures can be adopted for the promotion of the work, within or beyond the bounds of the

Conference; and what are the recommendations of Districts on this important subject?

A record of the proceedings of the Conference shall be kept by the Secretary, which shall be signed by the President and Secretary, and preserved among the documents of the Conference.

THE STATIONING COMMITTEE.

RULE I. The Stationing Committee shall consist of the President and Secretary of Conference, Co-Delegate, Missionary Secretaries, Chairmen of Districts, the President of Victoria College (being a member of the Conference), one member of the Conference from each District elected by ballot at its Annual Meeting, and the Ex-President, Ex-Secretary, and Ex-Co-Delegate.

RULE II. The Stationing Committee shall meet at the call of the President at the place appointed for holding the annual Conference, at least three days previous to the commencement of its sessions, to prepare a draft of the stations; which draft shall be printed and ready at the opening of the session, for the use of members of Conference.

RULE III. The Stationing Committee shall meet as often as may be deemed necessary during the sessions of the Conference, for the revision of the stations, and each member of Conference shall have the right to appear before the Committee to represent his case in regard to his appointment.

RULE IV. The distribution of the first draft of the Stations shall be regarded as a first reading; and by the second reading, which shall be not earlier than the second Wednesday of the Conference, the Stations shall be confirmed,

Rule V. The Stationing Committee shall not allow any Minister or Preacher to remain more than three years successively on the same Circuit or Station; except the Editor, Book Steward, Missionary Secretaries, Superannuated and Supernumerary Ministers, Missionaries among the Indians, and the Presidents, Principals, or Teachers of Seminaries of learning which are, or may be, under our superintendence.

Rule VI. As soon as the Stations are confirmed by the second reading, the Secretary shall read over successively the names of the Ministers stationed in each District, and the Conference shall elect by ballot one of the members of Conference so stationed, to be Chairman for the ensuing year.

Section II.

OF DISTRICT MEETINGS.

Ques. 1. What regulations are necessary for the preservation of our whole economy in active efficiency?

Ans. Let the work be divided into Districts.

Ques. 2. What regulations shall be made concerning the management of Districts?

Ans. The Chairman shall oversee all the spiritual and temporal business of the Church, in his District, and shall, in conjunction with the travelling Ministers and Preachers under his care, be responsible to the Conference for the execution of the Discipline.

Ques. 3. Who compose the District Meetings?

Ans. All members of Conference, and Preachers on trial in each District; and, when the financial affairs of the District are under consideration, the Recording Stewards of the several Circuits and Missions, and one other Lay-representative for each travelling Minister or Preacher appointed, in addition to the Superintendent on each Circuit or Mission.

Ques. 4. What directions shall be given concerning the District Meetings?

Ans. 1. After the Chairman has opened the Meeting by the usual devotional exercises, a Secretary shall be elected by ballot, who shall keep a record of the proceedings in a book procured for that purpose. At the close of each Meeting the Minutes shall be signed by the Chairman and Secretary. The book shall be kept by the Chairman, and brought to Conference; and delivered by him to his successor.

2. The method of proceeding at each Meeting shall be as follows:—The Chairman shall inquire:

First.—What members are now present?

Second.—Are the Ministers and Preachers blameless in life, conversation, and doctrine?

In the examination of Ministers and Preachers in the District Meeting, the Chairman is required to ask the following questions, *distinctively* and *successively*, concerning every brother:

1. Is there any objection to his moral and religious character?

2. Does he believe and preach all our doctrines?

3. Has he duly observed and enforced our discipline?

4. Has he been punctual in attending all his appointments?

5. Has he competent abilities for our itinerant work?

A separate answer to each of these questions is expected to appear on the District Minutes.

The Chairmen are required to examine into the case of every Minister who has married during the year, whether the fourth of the " Rules of a Preacher" has been obeyed, which says, "Take no steps towards marriage without first consulting your brethren;" and to report to the Conference any cases in which that important direction shall appear to have been violated. This rule shall be considered as requiring in particular a consultation with the Chairman of his District, his Superintendent, or some senior Minister competent to give advice in the case.

Third.—Who go to Conference?

The District Meetings respectively shall have the right of appointing the Ministers who are to attend the Conference, but they shall not exceed the number authorized annually by the Conference : and shall be subject to the following limitations, viz :—

1. Let not all the Ministers from any Circuit ever come to Conference, except from within such a distance of the place where it is held, as will admit of their supplying their places on the Lord's-day ; or except in very special cases, a majority of two-thirds of the District Meeting shall decide that all the brethren in any Circuit ought to attend.

2. Let those who attend set out as late, and return as early as possible; and in case of changes it is expected that the newly-appointed Ministers and Preachers will be on their respective Circuits not later than the first Sabbath in July; and those who retire shall be held responsible for the supply of the pulpits until that time.

3. Every Preacher on trial who has travelled four years, and been recommended by his District Meeting to the Conference to be admitted into full connection, shall attend the Conference of that year.

4. Nothing in these rules shall be so construed as to prevent those Ministers from attending the Conference, against whom there lies any accusation or complaint.

Fourth.—What Ministers are appointed by this Meeting to represent the District as members of Conference Committees? The Stationing? Church Relief? Sabbath School?

Fifth.—Are the young men on trial acquainted with the prescribed course of study, and what books have they read?

The Reports of Examining Committees are to be presented to the District Meetings for consideration; and their recommendation is to be recorded in the Minutes of the District, to be read at the Conference.

The Chairman shall also examine every Preacher on trial respecting his acquaintance with the books recommended to him, and the general course of reading which he has pursued during the preceding year. For this purpose every such Preacher is required to deliver to the Chairman of his District a list of the books which he has read since the preceding District Meeting. This list shall be laid before the Meeting, that the senior brethren may have an opportunity of giving to the junior Preachers such advice and directions respecting their studies as may appear necessary.

In addition to the preceding course of inquiry the following questions are to be put every year by the Chairman to every young man on the District on trial, but they need not be inserted in the District Minutes. It is enough to say that the usual questions were put to the young men on trial and satisfactorily answered; or, if otherwise, to state the case. In the Annual Examination of Candidates for our Ministry, it shall be the duty of the Chairmen of Districts to include the Disciplinary question, "Do you take snuff, tobacco, or drams?" and a distinct answer in the negative shall be required in every case as a condition of continuing on trial, from year to year.

1. Have you now faith in Christ, and are you going on to perfection?

2. Have you attended regularly to private prayer, and to the devotional reading of the Scriptures, and books of a spiritual and experimental kind, in order to keep up devout and lively religious feelings in your own heart?

3. Have you carefully visited the sick under your charge, and others to whom you could obtain access?

4. Have you visited the people at their houses, inquiring into their religious state, praying with them, and administering wholesome counsel; and have you catechised the children of the schools, and those of your friends and hearers, as you have had opportunity?

5. Have you had fruit of your ministry during the year, and are you endeavouring so to state the leading truths of Christian doctrine and experience in your discourses, and so to apply them with affection, and earnestness, and prayer, as to do all in your power to secure success in your work?

6. Answer the following questions in such terms as you would use in stating the doctrines they contain to an inquirer under religious impressions, or in your sermons:—What is Evangelical Repentance? What is Justification? What is Justifying Faith? What is the direct Witness of the Spirit? What is the indirect Witness of the Spirit? What is Christian Perfection? What is the difference between Justification and Sanctification? What is the difference between Justification and Regeneration? What is the difference between Sanctification and entire Sanctification?

Let these points be proved in order by appropriate passages of Holy Writ.

The brethren will see the propriety of conducting this part of the proceedings with peculiar deliberation and solemnity, as in the immediate presence of God; and they may enlarge on doctrinal questions as they may deem necessary, so as to lead the candidates to a right understanding, and an appropriate expression of our leading doctrinal peculiarities as a Church.

Sixth.—Who have travelled four years and are now recommended to the Conference to be received into full connexion and ordained?

Seventh.—What Preachers are recommended to be continued on trial?

1. Who have travelled *three* years?
2. Who have travelled *two* years?
3. Who have travelled *one* year?

Eighth.—What Preachers are on the List of Reserve?

Where the Preacher has been recommended to travel, but not called out into the work in the course of the year, the Chairman shall make inquiry of the Superintendent of the Circuit where he resides, whether he be still deemed a proper person to be employed in our regular ministry; and the result shall be reported to the District Meeting.

Ninth.—What Preachers are recommended to be received on trial?

The Chairmen are required not only to examine very minutely in the District Meetings all persons proposed as candidates for our Ministry, but also to report distinctly in their District Minutes, for the consideration of Conference, the opinion of the District Meetings after such examinations, respecting the health, piety, moral character, ministerial abilities, and educational acquirements, belief of our doctrines, attachment to our discipline, and freedom from debt, as well as from all secular encumbrances.

Ques. 1. How shall we try those who profess to be moved by the Holy Ghost to preach?

Ans. 1. Let the following questions be asked:—Do they know God as a pardoning God? Have they the love of God abiding in them? Do they desire nothing but God? And are they holy in all manner of conversation?

2. Have they gifts as well as grace for the work? Have they a clear, sound understanding—a right judgment in the things of God—a just conception of salvation by faith? And has God given them an acceptable way of speaking? Do they speak justly, readily, clearly?

3. Have they fruit? Are any truly convinced of sin, and converted to God by their preaching?

As long as these three marks concur in any one, we believe he is called of God to preach. These we receive as sufficient proof that he is moved by the Holy Ghost.

Ques. 2. How is a Preacher received on trial, and what regulations are observed respecting him during his probation?

Ans. 1. Before a Chairman or Superintendent shall propose a Preacher to the District Meeting to be recommended to the Conference to be admitted on trial, such Preacher must first be approved and recommended by the Quarterly Official Meeting of the Circuit or Station on which he resides.

2. Every candidate thus recommended shall attend the ensuing District Meeting, and be examined before all the brethren present respecting his religious experience, his knowledge of divine things, his educational acquirements, his reading, his views of the doctrines of the Gospel, and his regard for Methodism in general.

He shall also be required to have passed a satisfactory examination on the subjects prescribed by the Conference, as the preliminary Course of Study.

3. Every person proposed to the District Meeting is then to be asked by the Chairman the following questions, to each of which a distinct answer shall be required :—

Have you been converted to God? Have you been pardoned? Have you faith in Christ? Are you going on to perfection? Do you expect to be made perfect in love in this life? Are you groaning after it? Are you resolved to devote yourself wholly to God and his work? Have you been baptised? What are your views on Infant Baptism, and the Lord's Supper? Do you know the Rules of the Society? Do you keep them? Do you take snuff, tobacco, or drams? Have you read the whole Discipline? Are you willing to conform to it? Have you considered the twelve rules of a preacher, as contained in answer to question 2nd, Section IV., Chapter III., especially the first, the tenth, and the twelfth? 'Will you keep them for conscience sake? Are you determined to employ all your time in the work of God? Will you preach at every suitable opportunity, endeavouring not to speak too long or too loud? Will you diligently instruct the children in every place? Will you visit from house to house? Will you recommend fasting, both by precept and example? Are you in debt? What is your age? Have you good health, and have you a sound constitution? Are you engaged to marry?

Do you sincerely and fully believe the doctrines of Methodism as contained in our Articles of Faith, and as taught by Mr. Wesley in his notes on the New Testament and volumes of sermons?—especially the following leading ones—a Trinity of Persons in the Unity of the Godhead; the total depravity of all men by nature, in consequence of Adam's fall;

the Atonement made by Christ for the sins of all the human race; the direct witness of the Spirit; the possibility of falling from a state of justification and holiness, and perishing everlastingly; the absolute necessity of holiness, both in heart and life; and the proper eternity of future rewards and punishments? Will you endeavour fully and faithfully to preach them? What is your religious experience? and what is your call to this work?

4. After the examination the Candidate shall withdraw, and the Meeting shall determine whether he shall be recommended to the ensuing Conference to be received on trial.

5. If it be not convenient for the Candidate to attend the District Meeting, the Chairman with two other Ministers shall examine him as above directed, and report the result to the District Meeting.

6. If a Preacher who has been received on trial, but not into full connection, desist from travelling, he shall be dropped in silence, unless he desist from want of health.

7. A Preacher who marries while on trial shall be dropped in silence.

8. Observe: taking on trial is entirely different from admitting a Preacher into full connection. One on trial may be either admitted or rejected without doing him any wrong: otherwise it would have been no trial at all. Let every Chairman explain this to them on trial.

9. The time for a Preacher to remain on trial shall be four years, at the end of which period, if recommended by his District Meeting, he may be received into full connection.

10. Every Preacher on trial shall pursue the course of study prescribed by the Conference; and before he shall be received into full connection he shall give satisfactory evi-

dence to the District Meeting, from year to year, of his knowledge of the subjects and books included in such course of study.

11. After four years' probation, and an examination before, and approval by the Conference, he shall be received into full connection and be publicly recognized. If a Preacher who has been received on trial but not into full connection desist from want of health, or is proved guilty of immorality, it shall be stated in the Minutes; but in all other cases his name shall be dropped in silence.

12. All young men taken into the work by Chairmen of Districts, with the consent of the President, before the November Quarterly Official Meeting, shall be allowed the full year.

13. No Chairman of a District, or other Conference officer, shall have authority to employ a married Preacher during the year, with a view to his being received as a Candidate for our Ministry, without the consent of the Conference, or the Conference Special Committee.

14. No District Meeting shall recommend any married Preacher to the Conference for reception on trial, unless he has been previously employed, in case of absolute necessity, in accordance with the foregoing restriction.

15. When a Preacher's name is not inserted in the Minutes, he must receive a written license from the President, or the Chairman of the District on which he resides.

Tenth.—What Candidates for the Ministry are recommended to attend Victoria College during the year?

1. Before any Candidate for our Ministry shall be sent to College, his circumstances shall be inquired into by the District Meeting; and when such Preacher on trial is appointed to go to College by the Conference, the Minute of

the District Meeting in his case shall be forwarded to the Secretary of the Educational Fund Committee. No Candidate for our Ministry shall be sent to College who has not travelled at least one year.

2. When a Preacher on trial is allowed to attend Victoria College, for one or more years, his probation shall extend over five years at least, three of which shall be passed in Circuit work. Any Probationer assisted by the Educational Fund, who, within the period of ten years after Ordination, may wish to withdraw from the Conference, shall be required to refund the amount of aid given him, before receiving a certificate of standing, provided always that this requirement shall not apply to those who retire from ill health.

4. Preachers on trial who have graduated in arts, in any University, shall be exempt from examination in the Conference Course of Study, except in the subjects of Theology and Church History.

Eleventh.—What Ministers or Preachers have died ?

Twelfth.—Who are recommended as Superannuated Ministers ?

Thirteenth.—Who are recommended as Supernumerary Ministers ?

Fourteenth.—Who have desisted from Travelling ?

Fifteenth.—Who have been suspended during the year; and what is the recommendation of the District Meeting in the case ?

Sixteenth.—What is the number of our Church Members ? The number of Preaching-places and attendants on Public Worship, on each Circuit or Mission ? The number of Baptisms administered and Marriages solemnized by each Minister ? Have all such Marriages, solemnized during the year, been duly recorded, and the returns made according to law?

Seventeenth.—What is the number of Ministers' children on the District, having claims on the Children's Fund; and what are their respective names and ages? Have all the regulations respecting the Children's Fund been fully carried into effect in the District?

Eighteenth.—What is the number of Ministers, Preachers, and Laymen, in the Quarterly Official Meeting of each Circuit and Mission? Of Sabbath Schools? And what Connexional Property? Have the approved Conference Schedules been duly filled up?

Nineteenth.—Can any measures be adopted for increasing the efficiency of our ministerial labours, and the promotion of the work of God?

1. Are all the means possible used to visit all the towns and settlements within the boundaries of each Circuit or Mission?

2. Are there earnest attempts made in every place where there are services, to form classes?

3. Is sufficient time allotted in the arrangements of the Quarterly Visitation of the Classes for the Minister or Preacher to acquaint himself with the state of each member, and to give suitable advice to each?

4. Have the Rules of Society been read during the year, and have they been given to the members on trial, according to the Discipline?

5. Do the brethren pay sufficient attention to Pastoral visitation, and the catechising of the children of our members and friends?

Secondly. These important enquiries shall be followed by the reading of the Resolutions of the Conference held in

Belleville in 1836, (Minutes, page 120,) to be followed with a solemn review of the state of the work of God. And any suggestions for the religious improvement of our children and the members of our Church, and especially for the greater efficiency of our Ministerial labours, are to be entered on the Minutes of the District Meeting, and, when thought necessary, recommended to the consideration of the Conference.

Twentieth.—What Stewards and other Lay Representatives have been appointed by the several Circuits and Missions? Who are now present?

The Recording Stewards and other Lay Representatives, shall attend the District Meetings during the consideration of the financial affairs of the District, in order to lay before the meeting the accounts of their respective Circuits or Missions, and to confer with the Ministers and Preachers on the best means of promoting the interests of the Church. Let it be understood and announced for the Stewards and other Lay Representatives from the several Circuits and Missions to attend the District Meeting precisely at 10 o'clock on the morning of the second day of the Meeting, when the financial affairs of the District will be taken into consideration, during which the Stewards and other Lay Representatives shall have a right to speak and vote.

Twenty-first.—What are the Receipts and what is the Expenditure of each Circuit or Mission?

Twenty-second.—What has been collected on each Circuit and Mission for Connexional Funds? Have these been duly forwarded to their several Treasurers?

Twenty-third.—What special cases are now recommended to the favorable consideration of the several Connexional Funds? Church Relief—Churches? Contingent or Missionary—Circuits or Missions, Ministers or Preachers?

Twenty-fourth.—What Churches or Parsonages have been built, enlarged, or sold during the year? What Connexional Property is insured? In what Office? For how much? At what rates? What Parsonages have been furnished? What other Connexional Property has been acquired? What changes in relation to Church Property are now recommended? What property has been destroyed by fire?

Twenty-fifth.—What can be done to improve the financial state of the District?

1. Are all the financial arrangements of the Church duly observed in each Circuit and Mission? The Quarterly Contributions at the renewal of Tickets? The public collections and private subscriptions?

2. What changes are recommended in the order and arrangement of the work on the Circuits and Missions? What new Circuits or Missions are recommended? What additional Preachers are required for any Circuit or Mission on the District?

Twenty-sixth.—What Laymen are appointed by this Meeting as Members of the Conference Committees? The Church Relief? Contingent? Educational? and Missionary?

In the appointment of Laymen to our Conference Committees, the Chairman nominates out of those who have been chosen by the Quarterly Official Meetings, and only the Lay Members of the Meeting who may be present vote in their appointment, (except in the appointment of the Member of the Missionary Committee, in which case the Ministers and Laymen both vote).

Two copies of the District Meeting records shall be brought to Conference in addition to the one entered in the District Book:—One copy for the Secretary of Conference, and one for the members of the District and of the Conference.

FINANCIAL DISTRICT MEETINGS.

1. A Financial District Meeting, consisting of the Superintendent, and a Steward from each Circuit and Mission, shall be held in each District in the month of September, to apportion to the several Circuits the amounts placed at their disposal by the Conference; to make arrangements for Missionary Meetings, which arrangements shall be binding on all concerned; and to arrange the claims for the Ministers' children of the District.

2. The Financial District Meeting shall examine into the circumstances and probable income of the Domestic Missions, in the same way as they examine into those of the Circuits, and recommend the amount which, in their judgment, should be appropriated towards the support of such Missions; which shall be reported by the Chairman to the Missionary Secretaries.

3. The Financial Secretaries shall be the Local Treasurers of the District, and shall pay to the Superintendents of Circuits, or on their order, the sums appropriated to their Circuits, which payments such Superintendents shall report to their respective Quarterly Official Meetings.

Section III.

OF LOCAL PREACHERS AND THEIR MEETINGS.

Ques. 1. What directions shall be given concerning Local Preachers and their Meetings?

Ans. 1. Where there are six Local Preachers on a Circuit, of three years' continuous standing, the Superintendent shall regularly meet the Local Preachers once a quarter; and no person shall be put upon the plan as a Local Preacher, or be suffered to preach among us as such, without the approbation of that meeting, on the nomination of the Superintendent. Or, if in any Circuit such a Local Preachers' Meeting cannot be held, they shall be proposed and approved at the Quarterly Official Meeting of the Circuit.

2. The Superintendent at each regular Local Preachers' Meeting, or the Chairman or Superintendent at the last Quarterly Official Meeting of the Circuit, shall inquire into the religious and moral character, doctrines, abilities to preach, and punctuality in attending appointments, of each Preacher by name.

3. The questions proposed in the examination of the characters of Local Preachers, shall be the same as those proposed in regard to Travelling Preachers, viz :—

1. Is there any objection to his moral and religious character?
2. Does he believe and preach all our Doctrines?
3. Has he duly observed our Discipline?
4. Has he competent abilities for a Preacher?
5. Is he punctual in attending all his appointments?
6. Every person proposed to be received as a Local Preacher, or taken on trial, shall be asked by the Chairman or Superintendent the following questions, to which a distinct answer shall be required.

What is your religious experience? Have you faith in Christ? Are you going on to perfection? Do you expect to be perfected in love in this life? Are you groaning after it? Are you resolved to devote yourself to God and his work? Do you sincerely and fully believe the doctrines of Methodism as contained in our Articles of Faith, and as taught by Mr. Wesley in his Notes on the New Testament, and Volumes of Sermons?—especially the following leading ones: a Trinity of Persons in the Unity of the Godhead;

the total Depravity of all men by nature in consequence of Adam's fall; the Atonement made by Christ for the sins of all the human race; Justification by Faith; the direct Witness of the Spirit; the possibility of falling from a state of Justification and Holiness, and perishing everlastingly; the absolute necessity of holiness both in heart and life; and the proper eternity of rewards and punishments. What is Evangelical Repentance? What is Justification? What is Justifying Faith? What is the direct Witness of the Spirit? What is the indirect Witness of the Spirit? What is Christian Perfection? What is the difference between Justification and Sanctification? What is the difference between Justification and Regeneration? What is the difference between Sanctification and entire Sanctification?

2. Will you endeavour fully and faithfully to preach these doctrines?

3. All Local Preachers shall meet in class. No exception shall be made in respect to any who may have been Travelling Ministers or Preachers in former years.

4. No Local Preacher shall hold Love-feasts without the consent of the Superintendent, nor in any wise interfere with his business.

5. Whenever a Local Preacher or Exhorter removes from one Circuit to another, he shall obtain from the Superintendent of the Circuit a certificate of his official standing in the Church at the time of his removal, without which he shall not be received as a Local Preacher or Exhorter in other places.

6. No Local Preacher coming to reside among us from another part of the world, although duly recommended, shall be allowed to preach or hold meetings in our Churches unless he become a member of the Church and submit to its Discipline.

7. No Minister or Preacher who has been suspended or expelled by the Conference, shall on any account be employed as a Local Preacher without the consent of the Conference.

8. The name of every Local Preacher shall be recorded on the Journals of the Quarterly Official Meeting of the Circuit in which he resides.

9. Preachers who have been formerly in connection with the Conference, but who have located, shall be subject to all the regulations affecting Local Preachers, and when charged with immorality shall be proceeded against as other Local Preachers. The Superintendent of the Circuit shall report the case to the District Meeting.

10. Should any Local Preacher belonging to any seceding body of Methodists make application to be received into our Church, the Chairman of the District or Superintendent of the Circuit, in concurrence with the Quarterly or Local Preachers' Meeting of the Circuit on which such Local Preacher shall reside, is authorized to receive him, after having inquired into his qualifications and all the circumstances of his case.

Section IV.

OF QUARTERLY OFFICIAL MEETINGS.

Ques. 1. Of whom shall the Quarterly Official Meeting be composed?

Ans. Of all the Ministers, the Travelling and Local Preachers, Exhorters, Stewards, and Class Leaders of the Circuit or Mission.

Ques. 2. Who shall preside at the Quarterly Official Meetings?

Ans. The Chairman of the District, or in his absence the Superintendent of the Circuit.

Ques. 3. What shall be the regular business of the Quarterly Official Meeting?

Ans. 1. To receive the financial returns from the several classes, and to pay the salaries, allowances, and expenses of the Ministers and Preachers.

2. To hear complaints, and to receive and try appeals.

3. At the November Quarterly Official Meeting, to appoint the Stewards of the Circuit, the number to be not less than three, nor more than seven, one of whom shall be Recording Steward, who shall keep a record of the proceedings in a book procured for that purpose.

4. At the February Quarterly Official Meeting, to recommend candidates for the Ministry.

5. At the May Quarterly Official Meeting, to appoint a Committee, which shall meet after the Conference, to make an estimate of the amounts necessary for the family or families of the Ministers or Preachers of the Circuit, a report of which shall be made to the August Quarterly Official Meeting; and to appoint the Lay Representative or Representatives to attend the ensuing District Meeting.

6. Where there is no Local Preachers' Meeting, to enquire into the character, gifts, labors, punctuality and usefulness of each Local Preacher by name, and, if there be no valid objection alleged and sustained, to renew their licenses.

7. To examine the character of Exhorters, and annually, at the May Quarterly Meeting, to renew their licenses.

8. At any Quarterly Meeting, where there is no Local Preachers' Meeting, to license Local Preachers in case of necessity.

CHAPTER III.

MINISTERS, PREACHERS, AND THEIR DUTIES.

Section I.

OF THE APPOINTMENT OF PRESIDENTS AND THEIR DUTIES.

Ques. 1. How is a President to be appointed or chosen?
Ans. The English Conference shall have authority to send from year to year one of its own body, to be President of this Conference, or to appoint a member of this Conference to that office. When the English Conference does not send or appoint a President, or the President does not arrive, this Conference shall, on its assembling, choose by ballot one from amongst its own members; but the same individual shall not be re-chosen President oftener than once in four years, nor continue in office longer than one year at a time.

Ques. 2. What are the duties and powers of a President?
Ans. 1. To preside in the Conference, and in all Conference Connexional Committees; and give a casting vote in case of an equal division.

2. To see that the appointments of the Ministers and Preachers for the Districts, Circuits, Stations, and Missions, are made according to the rules of Conference respecting the Stationing Committee.

3. To ordain the Preachers received into full Connexion, with the assistance of two or more of the senior Ministers, according to our form of Ordination.

4. In the intervals of Conference, to travel through the Connexion at large, and oversee the spiritual and temporal business of the Church ; or be placed on a Circuit or Station, as the Stationing Committee or Conference may direct. The President shall be, *ex-officio*, Chairman of the District, for the time being, through which he may travel, or in which he may be stationed, during the year of his Presidency. He is also, *ex-officio*, Chairman of all Connexional Committees. Each President appointed by the English Conference, so long as he remains in the country, in the intervals of Conference, is expected to travel through the whole Connexion, so far as his circumstances will admit.

Ques. 3. To whom is the President amenable for his conduct ?

Ans. To the Conference ; and if he be accused of immorality in the interval of Conference, he shall be proceeded against in the District in which he is stationed or resides, or through which he may be travelling where the alleged crime is said to have been committed, in the same manner as against a Chairman of a District.

Ques. 4. How may we provide against the difficulties and inconveniences resulting from the death or disability of any President of the Conference during the year of his Presidency ?

Ans. 1. In every such case the Co-Delegate shall immediately enter into the office, and shall be considered as having all the powers, privileges, and authority of the President, and as being responsible for all his duties during the time of such disability, or absence from the country ; and in case of the death of the President, during the remainder of the year, and until the arrival or election of his successor at the commencement of the ensuing Conference.

2. And in the event of the death or disability of the President and Co-Delegate, the Secretary of the Conference shall call together the Conference Special Committee, which shall have power to appoint a President, who shall hold the office and discharge its duties until a successor is formally appointed at the next Conference.

Section II.

CHAIRMEN OF DISTRICTS AND THEIR DUTIES.

Ques. 1. Who is the Chairman ?

Ans. That Minister who oversees all the spiritual and temporal business of the Church in his District.

Ques. 2. By whom are the Chairmen of Districts to be chosen ?

Ans. By the Conference, according to the agreement between the English and Canadian Conferences, in 1858, which is in the following words :—" As soon as the stations are confirmed by a second reading of them to the Conference, the Secretary shall read over successively the names of the Ministers stationed in each District, and the Conference shall elect by ballot one of its members so stationed, to be Chairman for the ensuing year."

Ques. 3. What are the duties of a Chairman ?

Ans. 1. To take the oversight of the whole work on his District, according to the Discipline, as far as his duty to the Circuit on which he resides will permit.

2. To visit any Station or Circuit on his District when he may judge it expedient.

3. To see that every part of the Discipline is duly enforced. The Chairman is especially directed and required to visit any Circuit or Station in his District when requested by the Superintendent of such Circuit or Station, in case of any dispute or difficulty which the Superintendent may desire assistance to adjust; also, in all cases of appeal. In all these cases the Circuit or Station visited shall pay the travelling expenses of the Chairman. The Chairman shall have authority to call in any Minister or Preacher of his District to supply his place when absent in visiting any Circuit or Station.

4. In case of appeal on a Circuit or Station of which the Chairman is the Superintendent, the President shall either preside, or appoint the Co-Delegate, or a Chairman of a District to preside at the hearing of the appeal.

5. To preside in the District and Quarterly Official Meetings in his appointed District.

6. To take charge of all the Ministers, Travelling and Local Preachers and Exhorters in his District.

7. To change, receive, and suspend Ministers or Preachers in his District in the intervals of Conference, and in the absence of the President, as the Discipline directs: Provided, nevertheless, he shall not change any Minister or Preacher contrary to his wish, unless with the concurrence of two or more members of the Conference in his District.

8. If any Minister or Preacher absent himself from his Circuit without the leave of his Chairman, the Chairman shall, as far as possible, fill his place with another Minister or Preacher, who shall be paid for his labours out of the allowance of the absent Minister or Preacher, in proportion to the usual allowance.

9. To attend the President when present in his District, and to give him when absent all necessary information by letter of the state of his District.

10. Should the Chairman, or Superintendent, or any of his Colleagues, be requested to withdraw on any occasion from any of our regularly constituted meetings for business, he shall in no case do so; and should he be obliged to withdraw from any such meeting during its sittings, the meeting will be thereby dissolved. And if any Chairman, or Superintendent, or other Travelling Minister or Preacher do willingly submit to any requisition to withdraw from any such meeting before its conclusion, he shall, on proof, receive due censure at the ensuing Conference.

Ques. 4. Shall the Chairman have power to employ a Preacher who has been rejected at a previous Conference?

Ans. He shall not, unless the Conference give him liberty under certain conditions.

Ques. 5. What shall be done in the case of the death or disability of a Chairman during the year?

Ans. The Financial Secretary shall call a meeting of the members of the District, to elect, by ballot, one of their number, being a member of the Conference, as Chairman until the ensuing Conference.

Section III.

THE DUTIES OF SUPERINTENDENTS.

Ques. 1. Who is the Superintendent?

Ans. That Minister or Preacher on each Circuit who is appointed from time to time to take charge of the Ministers, Preachers, and Societies therein.

DUTIES OF SUPERINTENDENTS. 39

Ques. 2. What are the duties of the Superintendent?

Ans. 1. To see that the Ministers and Preachers in his Circuit behave well, and want nothing.

2. To renew the Tickets quarterly for the admission of members into Love-feast, and to regulate the Bands.

3. To enquire at the renewal of Tickets what each member can give for the Salary, and, when weekly money is not paid, what he can give for the Board of the Ministers and Preachers on the Circuit.

4. To meet the Stewards and Leaders regularly.

5. To appoint all the Leaders and change them, when he sees it necessary; but not contrary to the wish of the Class, or without consulting the Leaders' Meeting.

6. To receive, try, and expel Members, according to Discipline.

7. To hold Watch-nights and Love-feasts.

8. To hold Quarterly Meetings—to preside in all Official Meetings of the Circuit in the absence of the Chairman, and to make all nominations to office.

It shall be considered as a principle in Methodist Discipline that no court shall be recognized as Methodistic in which the Minister or Preacher does not preside.

9. To take care that every Society be duly supplied with books; and to urge upon all who are admitted into our Church to read attentively our General Rules, the Second Catechism, and other Wesleyan Works.

10. To take an exact account of the number of members in Society in his Circuit, and report to the District Meeting the number of members who have been received on trial, or by ticket, and of those who have removed, died, or ceased to be members, or have been separated from, or added to the Circuit by the alteration of its boundaries.

11. To leave for his successor a Circuit Book, containing a perfect list of all the official members, and also an exact list of the names of all the members in his Circuit, arranged in their classes, as found at the last Quarterly Official Meeting of the year.

12. To transmit to the Chairman his Quarterly Schedule, with such remarks as will furnish a full account of the state of the work under his charge.

13. To give due notice to the Chairman of the District in all cases of appeal.

Ques. 3. What other directions shall we give him ?

Ans. 1. To see that every Band-leader have the Rules of the Bands.

2. To enforce vigorously, but calmly, all the Rules of the Society.

3. To explain and enforce the General Rules of the Church, which are understood to prohibit our people from employing dancing-masters to teach their children to dance, or sending or allowing them to attend dancing-schools, or parties in which that amusement is practised.

4. To suffer no Love-feast to last above an hour and a half.

5. To remind members from time to time that none are to remove from one Circuit to another without a certificate of membership from a Minister of the Circuit, and to warn them that without such certificate they will not be received into the Church in other places; and also to forward a duplicate copy of such certificate by mail to the Superintendent of the Circuit to which they may be removing.

6. To recommend everywhere decency and cleanliness.

DUTIES OF SUPERINTENDENTS.

7. To see that the General Rules are read once a year in every Congregation, and occasionally in each Society, by himself or his colleague.

8. To appoint Prayer Meetings wherever he can in his Circuit, and to see that a fast be observed in every Society on the Friday preceding every Quarterly Meeting.

9. To license such persons as he may think proper to officiate as Exhorters, provided no person shall be so licensed without consulting the Stewards and Leaders, or Quarterly Official Meeting of the Circuit in which the person proposed resides.

10. To make a plan of appointments for the Ministers, the Travelling and Local Preachers, and Exhorters on the Circuit, with the counsel of the Local Preachers' Meeting, or of the Quarterly Official Meeting where there is no Local Preachers' Meeting.

11 To make strict inquiry in the Leaders' Meeting at least once a quarter into the moral character of all the Leaders, their punctuality in beginning and ending their Class Meetings in proper time, and whatever relates to their office.

12. To invite and earnestly urge the attendance and assistance of the Recording Stewards and other Lay Representatives at the District Meetings, according to our rule, during the time when the financial affairs of the District are under consideration.

13. To see that the circumstances of all remarkable deaths of our Church Members be drawn up and sent to our Editor, who may publish them as far as he judges proper.

14. To read, with the assistance of his colleague or colleagues, the Pastoral Address of the Conference to all the Societies in his Circuit.

15. To prepare and present to the District Meeting an Annual Report of the state of the Sabbath Schools in his Circuit.

16. To examine the accounts of all the Stewards.

17. To appoint a person to receive the Quarterly Collection in the Classes, if necessary.

18. To see that Mr. Wesley's original rule in regard to weekly and quarterly contributions be observed in all our Societies as far as possible. The rule was published by Mr. Wesley in the Minutes of Conference held in London, 1782. It is as follows:

"Q. Have all the weekly and quarterly contributions been made in all our Societies?

"A. In many it has been shamefully neglected. To remedy this—

"1. Let every Superintendent remind every Society that this was our original rule: Every member contributes one penny weekly (unless he is in extreme poverty), and one shilling quarterly. Explain the reasonableness of this.

"2. Let every Leader receive the weekly contribution from each person in his Class.

"3. Let the Superintendent ask every person at changing his Ticket: 'Can you afford to observe our rules?' And receive what he is able to give."

19. To see that all Public Collections in aid of the Circuit, or of the Connexional Funds, be regularly made in each Congregation of his Circuit.

20. To make application in the Classes, and to our friends, on behalf of the Superannuation Fund, during the months of November and December, and to pay the moneys thus received to the Financial Secretary, in time for transmission to the Treasurer on or before the first day of January.

21. To see that Collections for our Connexional Funds be taken up at the following times, viz. :
1. *Church Relief*, in the month of July.
2. *Contingent*, in the months of September and March.
3. *Educational*, in the month of December.

22. To carry out the arrangements made by the Financial District Meeting in regard to the Missionary work on his Circuit.

23. To pay promptly to the appointed Treasurers all money collected for the several Funds at the times directed by Conference.

Section IV.

OF THE DUTY OF TRAVELLING PREACHERS.

Ques. 1. What is the duty of a Preacher ?

Ans. 1. To preach. 2. To meet the Societies, Classes, and general Bands. 3. To visit the sick. 4. To preach in the morning where he can get hearers. We recommend morning preaching at five o'clock in the summer and six in the winter, wherever it is practicable.

Ques. 2. What are the directions given to a Preacher ?

Ans. 1. Be diligent. Never be unemployed, never be triflingly employed. Never trifle away time ; neither spend any more time at any place than is strictly necessary.

2. Be serious. Let your motto be, Holiness to the Lord. Avoid all lightness, jesting, and foolish talking.

3. Converse sparingly ; and conduct yourself prudently with women. 1 Tim. 5, 2.

4. Take no step towards marriage without first consulting your brethren.

5. Believe evil of no one without good evidence: unless you see it done, take heed how you credit it. Put the best construction on every thing. You know the judge is always supposed to be on the prisoner's side.

6. Speak evil of no one: because *your* word especially would eat as doth a canker. Keep your thoughts within your own breast, till you come to the person concerned.

7. Tell every one under your care what you think wrong in his conduct and temper, and that lovingly and plainly, as soon as may be, else it will fester in your heart. Make all haste to cast the fire out of your bosom.

8. Avoid all affectation. A Preacher of the Gospel is the servant of all.

9. Be ashamed of nothing but sin.

10. Be punctual. Do every thing exactly at the time. And do not mend our rules, but keep them, not for wrath, but for conscience sake.

11. You have nothing to do but save souls: Therefore spend and be spent in this work; and go always not only to those who want you, but to those who want you *most*.

Observe: It is not your business only to preach so many times, and to take care of this or that Society, but to save as many as you can—to bring as many sinners as you can to repentance, and with all your power to build them up in that holiness without which they cannot see the Lord. And remember—a Methodist Preacher is to mind every point, great and small, in the Methodist Discipline. Therefore you will need to exercise all the sense and grace you have.

12. Act in all things not according to your own will,

but as a son in the Gospel. As such it is your duty to employ your time in the manner which we direct; in preaching and visiting from house to house—in reading, meditation, and prayer. Above all, if you labour with us in the Lord's vineyard, it is needful you should do that part of the work which *we advise*, at the times and places which *we judge* most for his glory.

Section V.

OF THE ELECTION AND ORDINATION OF MINISTERS, AND THEIR DUTIES.

Ques. 1. How is a Minister constituted?

Ans. By election of the Conference, and by the laying on of the hands of the President and other senior Ministers.

Ques. 2. What are the duties of a Minister?

Ans. To conduct all parts of Divine worship, to administer Baptism and the Lord's Supper, to solemnize Matrimony, and in general to perform all the work of a Christian Minister.

No Minister who ceases to travel without the consent of the Conference, certified under the hand of the President, except in case of sickness, debility, or other unavoidable circumstances, shall, on any account, exercise the peculiar functions of his office, or even be allowed to preach among us; nevertheless, the final determination in all such cases is with the Conference.

Section VI.

OF THE RECEPTION OF MINISTERS FROM OTHER CHURCHES.

Ques. 1. On what condition shall we receive those Ministers who may come to us from the Wesleyan Connexion in Europe, the Affiliated Conferences, and the Methodist Episcopal Church in the United States?

Ans. If they come to us properly accredited from any of those Conferences, they may be received according to such credentials, provided they give satisfaction to the Conference of their willingness to conform to our church government and usages.

Ques. 2. How shall we receive Ministers who may offer to unite with us from any seceding Body of Methodists, or from other Christian Churches?

Ans. They may be received by the Conference, according to our usages, on condition of taking upon them our ordination vows, without re-imposition of hands, having previously given satisfaction to a committee composed of the Chairman and two other Ministers of the District, and to the Conference, of their being in Orders, and of their agreement with our Church in doctrine and discipline, government and usages; provided also that the Conference is satisfied with their gifts, grace, and usefulness.

Ques. 3. How shall we receive Preachers from any seceeding Body of Methodists, or from other Evangelical Denominations?

Ans. They may be received as Probationers, provided they give satisfaction that they are suitable persons to exercise the office; that they believe in the doctrines, and approve of the Discipline, government, and usages of our Church. The Chairman and any two Ministers (members of the Conference) of the District, within the bounds of which such Preacher may be travelling or resident, are authorised to act as a committee on behalf of the Conference, to admit him into our Church; and he may be employed until the ensuing Conference; and if he be recommended by a District Meeting he may be received as a Preacher on trial.

Section VII.

RULES BY WHICH WE SHOULD CONTINUE OR DESIST FROM PREACHING AT ANY PLACE.

Ques. 1. Is it advisable for us to preach in as many places as we can without forming any Societies?

Ans. By no means: we have made the trial in various places: and that for a considerable time. But all the seed has fallen by the way side. There is scarce any fruit remaining.

Ques. 2. Where should we endeavour to preach most?

Ans. 1. Where there is the greatest number of quiet and willing hearers.

2. Where there is most fruit.

Ques. 3. Ought we not diligently to observe in what places God is pleased at any time to pour out His Spirit more abundantly?

Ans. We ought: and at that time to send more labourers than usual into that part of the harvest.

Section VIII.

OF THE MATTER AND MANNER OF PREACHING, AND OF OTHER PUBLIC EXERCISES.

Ques. 1. What is the best general method of Preaching?

Ans. 1. To convince: 2. To offer Christ: 3. To invite: 4. To build up: And to do this in some measure in every sermon.

Ques. 2. What is the most effectual way of preaching Christ?

Ans. The most effectual way of preaching Christ, is to preach him in all his offices; and to declare his law, as well as his gospel, both to believers and unbelievers. Let us strongly and closely insist upon inward and outward holiness in all its branches.

Ques. 3. Are there any other advices which might be of use to us?

Ans. Perhaps these: 1. Be sure never to disappoint a congregation. 2. Begin at the time appointed. 3. Let your whole deportment be serious, weighty, and solemn. 4. Always suit your subject to your audience. 5. Choose the plainest text you can. 6. Take care not to ramble, but keep to your text, and make out what you take in hand. 7. Beware of anything awkward or affected, either in your gesture, phrase, or pronunciation. 8. Do not usually pray *extempore* above eight or ten minutes (at most) without intermission. 9. Frequently read and enlarge upon a portion of Scripture; and let young Preachers often exhort without taking a text. 10. Always avail yourselves of the great festivals, by preaching on such occasions.

Section IX.

OF THE DUTIES OF MINISTERS AND PREACHERS TO GOD, THEMSELVES, AND ONE ANOTHER.

Ques. 1. How shall the Minister or Preacher be qualified for his charge?

Ans. By walking closely with God, and having his work greatly at heart; and by understanding and loving discipline, ours in particular.

Ques. 2. Do we sufficiently watch over each other?

Ans. We do not. Should we not frequently ask each other: Do you walk closely with God? Have you now fellowship with the Father and Son? At what hour do you rise? Do you punctually observe the morning and evening hour of retirement? Do you spend the day in the manner which the Conference advises? Do you converse seriously, usefully, and closely? To be more particular: Do you use all the means of grace yourself, and enforce the use of them on all other persons? They are either instituted or prudential.

First.—The instituted are:

1. Prayer:—Private, family, and public; consisting of deprecation, petition, intercession, and thanksgiving. Do you use each of these? Do you forecast daily wherever you are, to secure time for private devotion? Do you practise it everywhere? Do you ask everywhere—Have you family prayer? Do you ask individuals—Do you use private prayer, every morning and evening in particular?

2. Searching the Scriptures by—

(1) Reading: *Constantly*, some part of them every day; *regularly*, all the Bible in order; *carefully*, with notes;

seriously, with prayer before and after; *fruitfully*, immediately practising what you learn there.

(2) Meditating: At set times. By rule.

(3) Hearing: Every opportunity; with prayer before, at, and after. Have you a Bible always about you?

3. The Lord's Supper: Do you use this at every opportunity? With solemn prayer before? With earnest and deliberate self-devotion?

4. Fasting: Do you use as much abstinence and fasting every week, as your health, strength, and labour will permit?

5. Christian Conference: Are you convinced how important and how difficult it is to order your conversation aright? Is it always with grace? Seasoned with salt? Meet to minister grace to the hearers? Do you not converse too long at a time? Is not an hour commonly enough? Would it not be well always to have a determinate end in view? And to pray before and after it?

Second.—Prudential means, we may use either as Christians, as Methodists, or as Ministers and Preachers.

1. As Christians: What particular rules have you in order to grow in grace? What arts of holy living?

2. As Methodists: Do you never miss your Class or Band?

3. As Ministers and Preachers: Have you thoroughly considered your duty? And do you make a conscience of executing every part of it? Do you meet every Society? Also, the Leaders and Bands?

These means may be used without fruit. But there are some means which cannot, namely, watching, denying ourselves, taking up our cross, exercise of the presence of God.

1. Do you steadily watch against the world? Yourself? Your besetting sin?

2. Do you deny yourself every useless pleasure of sense? Imagination? Honour? Are you temperate in all things? Instance in food: 1. Do you use only that kind and that degree which is best both for body and soul? Do you see the necessity of this? 2. Do you eat no more at each meal than is necessary? Are you not heavy and drowsy after dinner? 3. Do you use only that kind and that degree of drink which is best both for your body and soul? 4. Do you choose and use water for your drink? And only take wine medicinally or sacramentally?

3. Wherein do you take up your cross daily? Do you cheerfully bear your cross, however grievous, to profit thereby?

4. Do you endeavour to set God always before you? To see his eye continually fixed upon you? Never can you use these means but a blessing will ensue. And the more you use them, the more you will grow in grace.

Section X.

OF VISITING FROM HOUSE TO HOUSE, AND ENFORCING PRACTICAL RELIGION.

Ques. 1. How can we further assist those under our care?

Ans. 1. By instructing them at their own houses. What unspeakable need is there for this! The world says, "*The Methodists are no better than other people.*" This is not true in general; but, 1. Personal religion, either toward God or man, is too superficial among us. We can but just touch on a few particulars. How little faith is there among us!

How little communion with God, how little living in heaven, walking in eternity, deadness to every creature! How much love of the world! Desire of pleasure, of ease, of getting money! How little brotherly love! What continual judging one another! What gossiping, evil speaking, tale bearing! What want of moral honesty! To instance only one particular: Who does as he would be done by, in buying and selling?

2. Family religion is wanting in many branches. And what avails public preaching alone, though we could preach like angels? We must, yea, every Travelling Preacher must instruct the people from house to house! Till this is done, and that in good earnest, the Methodists will be no better.

Our religion is not sufficiently deep, universal, uniform: but superficial, partial, uneven. It will be so till we spend half as much time in this visiting, as we now do in talking uselessly. Can we find a better method of doing this than Mr. Baxter's? If not, let us adopt it without delay. His whole tract, entitled *Gildas Salvianus; or, The Reformed Pastor*, is well worth a careful perusal. Speaking of this visiting from house to house, he says, (p. 351), "We shall find many hindrances, both in ourselves and the people."

1. In ourselves there is much dullness and laziness, so that there will be much ado to get us to be faithful in the work.

2. We have a base man-pleasing temper, so that we let them perish rather than lose their love; we let them go quietly to hell, lest we should offend them.

3. Some of us have a foolish bashfulness; we know not how to begin, and blush to contradict the devil.

4. But the great hindrance is weakness of faith. Our whole motion is weak because the spring is weak.

5. Lastly, we are unskilful in the work. How few know how to deal with men, so as to get within them, and suit all our discourse to their several conditions and tempers: to choose the fittest subjects, and follow them with a holy mixture of seriousness, terror, love, and meekness!

But undoubtedly this private application is implied in those solemn words of the Apostle, "*I charge thee therefore before God and the Lord Jesus Christ, who shall judge the quick and the dead at his appearing, and his kingdom, preach the word; be instant in season; out of season; reprove, rebuke, exhort, with all long-suffering, and doctrine.*"

O brethren, if we could but set this work on foot in all our societies, and prosecute it zealously, what glory would redound to God! If the common lukewarmness were banished, and every shop and every house busied in speaking of the word and works of God; surely God would dwell in our habitations, and make us his delight.

And this is absolutely necessary to the welfare of our people, some of whom neither repent nor believe to this day. Look around, and see how many of them are still in apparent danger of damnation. And how can you walk and talk, and be merry with such people, when you know their case! When you look them in the face you should break forth into tears, as the Prophet did when he looked upon Hazael, and then set on them with the most vehement exhortations. O, for God's sake, and the sake of poor souls, bestir yourselves, and spare no pains that may conduce to their salvation!

What cause have we to bleed before the Lord that we have so long neglected this good work! If we had but engaged in it sooner, how many more might have been brought to Christ! And how much holier and happier might our Societies have been before now! And why might we not have done it sooner? There were many hindrances: and so there always will be. But the greatest hindrance is in ourselves, in our littleness of faith and love.

But it is objected, I. "This will take up so much time we shall not have leisure to follow our studies." We answer, 1. Gaining knowledge is a good thing, but saving souls is a better. 2. By this very thing you will gain the most excellent knowledge, that of God and eternity. 3. You will have time for gaining other knowledge, too. Only sleep not more than you need; "and never be idle, or triflingly employed." But, 4. If you can do but one, let your studies alone. We ought to throw by all the libraries in the world, rather than be guilty of the loss of one soul.

It is objected, II. "The people will not submit to it." If some will not, others will. And the success with them will repay all your labour. O let us herein follow the example of St. Paul. 1. For our general business, *Serving the Lord with all humility of mind:* 2. Our special work, *Take heed to yourselves and to all the flock:* 3. Our doctrine, *Repentance towards God, and faith towards our Lord Jesus Christ:* 4. The place, *I have taught you publicly, and from house to house:* 5. The object and manner of teaching, *I ceased not to warn every one, night and day, with tears:* 6. His innocence and self-denial, *Herein have I coveted no man's silver or gold:* 7. His patience, *Neither count I my life dear unto myself.* And among all other motives, let these be ever before our eyes; 1. *The Church of God, which he hath purchased with his own blood.* 2. *Grievous wolves shall enter in; yea, of yourselves shall men arise speaking perverse things.*

Write this upon your hearts, and it will do you more good than twenty years' study. Then you will have no time to spare: you will have work enough. Then, likewise, no Preacher will stay with us who is as salt that has lost its savour. For to such this employment would be mere drudgery. And in order to it, you will have need of all the knowledge you can procure, and all the grace you can attain.

The sum is, go into every house in course, and teach all therein, both young and old, to be Christians inwardly and outwardly; make every particular plain to their understanding; fix it in their minds; write it on their hearts. In order to this, there must be line upon line, precept upon precept. What patience, what love, what knowledge is requisite for this! We must needs do this, were it only to avoid idleness. Do we not loiter away many hours in every week? Each try himself. No idleness is consistent with a growth in grace. Nay, without exactness in redeeming time, you cannot retain the grace you receive in justification.

Ques. 2. Why are we not more holy? Why do we not live in eternity? Walk with God all the day long? Why are we not all devoted to God? Breathing the whole spirit of Missionaries?

Ans. Chiefly because we are enthusiasts; looking for the end, without using any means. To touch only upon two or three instances. Who of us rise at four, or even at five, when we do not preach? Do we know the obligation and benefit of fasting, or abstinence? How often do we practise it? The neglect of this alone is sufficient to account for our feebleness and faintness of spirit. We are continually grieving the Holy Spirit of God by the habitual neglect of a plain duty. Let us amend from this hour.

Ques. 3. How should we guard against Sabbath-breaking, evil-speaking, unprofitable conversation, lightness, expensiveness or gaiety of apparel, and contracting debts without due care to discharge them?

Ans. 1. Let us preach expressly on each of these heads. 2. Read in every Society the sermon on evil speaking. 3. Let the Leaders closely examine and exhort every person to put away the accursed thing. 4. Let the Ministers and Preachers warn every Society, that none who is guilty herein can remain with us. 5. Extirpate out of our Church buying or selling goods which have not paid the duty laid upon them by Government. Let none remain with us who will not totally abstain from this evil in every kind and degree. Extirpate bribery,—receiving anything directly or indirectly,—for voting at any election. Show no respect to persons herein, but expel all that touch the accursed thing. And strongly advise our people to discountenance all treats given by candidates before or at elections, and not to be partakers, in any respect, of such iniquitous practices.

Section XI.

OF EMPLOYING OUR TIME PROFITABLY, WHEN NOT ENGAGED IN PUBLIC EXERCISES.

Ques. 1. What general method of employing our time shall we advise?

Ans. We advise, 1. As often as possible to rise at four. 2. From four to five in the morning, and from five to six in the evening, to meditate, pray, and read the Scriptures with notes, and the closely practical parts of what Mr. Wesley has published. 3. From six in the morning till twelve (allowing an hour for breakfast), read, with much prayer, some of our best religious books.

Ques. 2. Why is it that the people under our care are not better ?

Ans. Other reasons may concur, but the chief is, because we are not more knowing and more holy.

Ques. 3. But why are we not more knowing?

Ans. Because we are idle. We forgot our first rule, "Be diligent—never be unemployed—never be triflingly employed. Neither spend any more time at any place than is strictly necessary." We fear there is altogether a fault in this matter, and that few of us are clear. Which of us spend as many hours a day in God's work, as we did formerly in man's work? We talk, talk—or read what comes next to hand. We must, absolutely must, cure this evil or betray the cause of God. But how? 1. Read the most useful books, and that regularly and constantly. 2 Steadily spend all the morning in this employment, or at least five hours in four-and-twenty. "But I have no taste for reading." Contract a taste for it by use, or return to your former employment. "I have no books." Be diligent to spread the books, and you will have the use of them.

Section XII.

OF THE NECESSITY OF UNION AMONG OURSELVES.

Let us be deeply sensible (from what we have known) of the evil of a division in principle, spirit, or practice, and the dreadful consequences to ourselves and others. If we are united, what can stand before us? If we divide, we shall destroy ourselves, the work of God, and the souls of our people.

Ques. What can be done in order to a closer union with each other?

Ans. 1. Let us be deeply convinced of the absolute necessity of it.

2. Pray earnestly for and speak freely to each other.

3. When we meet, let us never part without prayer.

4. Take great care not to despise each other's gifts.

5. Never speak lightly of each other.

6. Let us defend each other's character in every thing, so far as is consistent with the truth.

7. Labour, in honour, each to prefer the other before himself.

8. We recommend a serious perusal of *The Causes, Evils, and Cures of the Heart and Church Divisions.*

Section XIII.

OF THE RELATION OF BAPTIZED CHILDREN TO THE CHURCH.

Ques. 1. Are all young children entitled to baptism?

Ans. We hold that all children, by virtue of the unconditional benefits of the atonement, are members of the kingdom of God, and, therefore, graciously entitled to baptism; but as infant baptism contemplates a course of religious instruction and discipline, it is expected of all parents or guardians who present their children for baptism, that they use all diligence in bringing them up in conformity to the word of God, and they should be solemnly admonished of this obligation, and earnestly exhorted to faithfulness therein.

Ques. 2. What is the relation of baptized children to the Church?

Ans. We regard all children who have been baptized, as placed in visible covenant relation to God, and under the special care and supervision of the Church.

Ques. 3. What shall be done for the children of our Congregations?

Ans. 1. Urge upon all parents the duty and importance of presenting their children to God in the ordinance of baptism.

2. As early as they shall be able to understand, let them be taught the nature, the design, and the obligations of their baptism, and the truths of religion necessary to make them wise unto salvation; let our Catechisms be placed in their hands, and let all who can, read and commit the same to memory; let them be encouraged to attend class, and to give regular attendance upon all the means of grace, according to their age, capacity, and religious experience.

3. Pray earnestly for them, and talk with them at every suitable opportunity.

4. As far as practicable, it shall be the duty of every Minister and Preacher to obtain the names of the children of his congregation, to form them into classes, for the purpose of giving them religious instruction, to instruct them regularly himself, as his other duties will allow; to appoint a suitable Leader for each class, who shall instruct them in his absence, and to leave for his successor a correct list of each class with the name of its Leader.

5. Preach expressly on education. "But I have no gift

for this." Pray earnestly for the gift, and use every other means to attain it.

6. Whenever a baptized child shall, by orphanage or otherwise, be deprived of Christian guardianship, the Superintendent shall ascertain and report to the Leaders' Meeting the facts in the case; and such provision shall be made for the Christian training of the child, as the circumstances of the case admit and require.

Section XIV.

OF PUBLIC WORSHIP.

Ques. 1. What direction shall be given for the establishment of uniformity in public worship among us, on the Lord's Day?

Ans. 1. Let the morning service consist of singing, prayer, the reading of a chapter out of the Old Testament and another out of the New, and preaching.

2. Let the afternoon and evening services consist of singing, prayer, the reading of one or two chapters out of the Bible, and preaching.

3. Let the Lord's Prayer also be used on all occasions of public worship in concluding the first prayer, and the Apostolic benediction in dismissing the congregation.

4. In administering the ordinances, let the form in the Discipline be used.

5. Let the Society be met, at least once a quarter, wherever it is practicable, on the Sabbath-day.

Ques. 2. Is there not a great indecency sometimes practised among us, viz., talking in the congregation before and after service? How shall this be cured?

Ans. Let the Ministers and Preachers enlarge on the impropriety of talking before or after service; and strongly exhort those that are concerned to do it no more.

Section XV.

OF THE SACRAMENTS.

BAPTISM.

1. Let every adult person, and the parents of every child to be baptized, have the choice either of sprinkling, pouring, or immersion, and wherever practicable, let the ordinance be administered in the public congregation.

2. Re-baptism, whether of those baptized in infancy or adult age, is entirely inconsistent with the nature and design of baptism, as set forth in the New Testament.

THE LORD'S SUPPER.

Ques. Are there any directions to be given concerning the administration of the Lord's Supper?

Ans. 1. Let those who have scruples concerning the receiving of it kneeling, be permitted to receive it either standing or sitting.

2. Let no person who is not a Member of our Church be habitually admitted to the communion, without examination, and some token given by the Minister.

3. No person shall be admitted to the Lord's Supper among us, who is guilty of any practice for which we would exclude a Member of our Church.

Section XVI.

OF THE SPIRIT AND TRUTH OF SINGING.

Ques. How shall we guard against formality in singing?

Ans. 1. By choosing such hymns as are proper for the congregation.

2. By not singing too much at once; seldom more than five or six verses.

3. By suiting the tune to the words.

4. By often stopping short, and asking the people, "Now! do you know what you said last? Did you speak no more than you felt?"

5. Do not suffer the people to sing too slowly. This naturally tends to formality, and is brought in by those who have either very strong or very weak voices.

6. In every large Society let them learn to sing; and let them always learn our tunes first.

7. Introduce no new tune till they are perfect in the old.

8. Recommend our tune book. And if you cannot sing yourself, choose a person or two at each place to pitch the tune for you.

9. Exhort every person in the congregation to sing; not one in ten only.

10. The singing and all other parts of public worship are under the control and direction of the Superintendent of the Circuit.

CHAPTER IV.

OF MEMBERS OF THE CHURCH.

Section I.

THE ORIGIN, DESIGN, AND GENERAL RULES OF OUR UNITED SOCIETIES.

1. In the latter end of the year 1739, eight or ten persons came to Mr. Wesley, in London, who appeared to be deeply convinced of sin, and earnestly groaning for redemption. They desired (as did two or three more the next day) that he would spend some time with them in prayer, and advise them how to flee from the wrath to come, which they saw continually hanging over their heads. That he might have more time for this great work, he appointed a day when they might all come together, which from thenceforward they did every week, namely, on *Thursday*, in the evening. To these, and as many more as desired to join with them, (for their numbers increased daily), he gave those advices, from time to time, which he judged most needful for them; and they always concluded their meetings with prayer, suited to their several necessities.

2. This was the rise of the UNITED SOCIETY, first in Europe and then in America. Such a Society is no other

than "*a company of men, having the form and seeking the power of godliness; united in order to pray together, to receive the word of exhortation, and to watch over one another in love, that they may help each other to work out their salvation.*"

3. That it may the more easily be discerned, whether they are indeed working out their own salvation, each Society is divided into smaller companies, called Classes, according to their respective places of abode. There are about twelve persons in a Class, one of whom is styled, *The Leader.* It is his duty,

First. To see each person in his Class once a week at least, in order,

1. To inquire how their souls prosper.
2. To advise, reprove, comfort, or exhort, as occasion may require.
3. To receive what they are willing to give, towards the support of the Ministers, Preachers, Church, and Poor.

Second. To meet the Ministers and Stewards of the Society once a week, in order,

1. To inform the Minister of any that are sick, or of any that walk disorderly and will not be reproved.
2. To pay the Stewards what they have received of the several Classes in the week preceding.

4. There is only one condition previously required of those who desire admission into these Societies,—*a desire to flee from the wrath to come, and be saved from their sins.*

But wherever this is really fixed in the soul, it will be shown by its fruits. It is therefore expected of all who continue therein, that they should continue to evidence their desire of salvation,

First. By doing no harm, by avoiding evil of every kind, especially that which is most generally practised,—such as :

The taking of the name of God in vain.

The profaning of the day of the Lord, either by doing ordinary work therein, or by buying or selling.

Drunkenness, buying or selling spirituous liquors, or drinking them, unless in cases of extreme necessity.

The buying and selling of men, women, and children, with the intention to enslave them.

Fighting, quarrelling, brawling, brother going to law with brother; returning evil for evil, or railing for railing; the using many words in buying or selling.

The buying or selling goods that have not paid the duty.

The giving or taking on usury, *i. e.,* unlawful interest.

Uncharitable or unprofitable conversation; particularly speaking evil of Magistrates or Ministers.

Doing to others as we would not they should do unto us.

Doing what we know is not for the glory of God,—as :

The putting on of gold or costly apparel.

The taking such diversions as cannot be used in the name of the Lord Jesus.

The singing those songs or reading those books which do not tend to the knowledge or love of God.

Softness and needless self indulgence.

Laying up treasure upon earth.

Borrowing without a probability of paying, or taking up goods without a probability of paying for them.

5. It is expected of all who continue in these Societies that they should continue to evidence their desire of salvation.

Secondly. By doing good, by being in every kind merciful after their power, as they have opportunity, doing good of every possible sort, and, as far as possible, to all men.

To their bodies, of the ability which God giveth, by giving food to the hungry, by clothing the naked, by visiting or helping them that are sick or in prison.

To their souls, by instructing, reproving, or exhorting all we have any intercourse with; trampling under foot that enthusiastic doctrine, that " we are not to do good, *unless our hearts are free to it.*"

By doing good, especially to them that are of the household of faith, or groaning so to be; employing them preferably to others; buying one of another; helping each other in business; and so much the more, because the world will love its own, and them only.

By all possible diligence and frugality, that the gospel be not blamed.

By running with patience the race which is set before them, denying themselves, and taking up their cross daily; submitting to bear the reproach of Christ, to be as of the filth and offscouring of the world; and looking that men should say all manner of evil of them *falsely for the Lord's sake.*

6. It is expected of all who desire to continue in these Societies that they should continue to evidence their desire of salvation.

Thirdly. By attending to all the ordinances of God,—such as:

The public worship of God.
The ministry of the word, either read or expounded.
The Supper of the Lord.
Family and private prayer.
Searching the Scriptures, and
Fasting or abstinence.

7. These are the general rules of our Societies; all of

which we are taught of God to observe, even in his written word, *which is the only rule, and the sufficient rule, both of our faith and practice.* And all these we know his Spirit writes on truly awakened hearts. If there be any among us who observe them not, who habitually break any of them, let it be known unto them who watch over that soul, as they who must give an account. We will admonish him of the error of his ways. We will bear with him for a season. But, if then he repent not, he hath no more place among us. We have delivered our own souls.

Section II.

OF THE BAND SOCIETIES.

Two, three, or four true believers, who have confidence in each other, form a band :—only it is to be observed, that in each of these bands, all must be men, or all women; and all married, or all unmarried.

Rules of the Band Societies, drawn up December 25, 1738.

The design of our meeting is to obey that command of God, *Confess your faults one to another, and pray one for another, that ye may be healed.*—James v. 16.

To this end we agree,—

1. To meet once a week at least.
2. To come punctually at the hour appointed; unless some extraordinary reason prevents.
3. To begin exactly at the hour with singing or prayer.
4. To speak, each of us in order, freely and plainly, the true state of our souls, with the faults we have committed

in tempers, words, or actions, and the temptations we have felt since our last meeting.

5. To end every meeting with prayer, suited to the state of each person present.

6. To desire some person among us to speak his own state first, and then to ask the rest in order, as many and as searching questions as may be, concerning their state, sins, and temptations.

Some of the questions proposed to one before he is admitted among us may be to this effect :—

1. Have you the forgiveness of your sins ?

2. Have you peace with GOD, through Our LORD JESUS CHRIST ?

3. Have you the witness of God's Spirit with your spirit that you are a child of God ?

4. Is the love of God shed abroad in your heart ?

5. Has no sin, inward or outward, dominion over you ?

6. Do you desire to be told of your faults ?

7. Do you desire to be told of *all* your faults, and that plain and home ?

8. Do you desire that every one of us should tell you, from time to time, whatsoever is in his heart concerning you ?

9. Consider ! Do you desire we should tell you whatsoever we hear concerning you ?

10. Do you desire that in doing this we should come as close as possible, that we should cut to the quick, and search your heart to the bottom ?

11. Is it your desire and design to be on this, and all other occasions, entirely open, so as to speak without disguise and without reserve ?

Any of the preceding questions may be asked as often as occasion requires ; the four following at every meeting :

1. What known sins have you committed since our last meeting?
2. What particular temptations have you met with?
3. How were you delivered?
4. What have you thought, said, or done, of which you doubt whether it be sin or not?

Directions given to the Band Society, December 25th, 1744.

You are supposed to have the *Faith that overcometh the world.* To you, therefore, it is not grievous,

I. Carefully to abstain from doing evil; in particular,

1. To neither *buy* nor *sell* anything at all on the Lord's-day.
2. To taste no spirituous liquor, no dram of any kind, unless prescribed by a physician.
3. To be *at a word* in buying or selling.
4. Not to mention the *faults* of any *behind his back,* and to stop those short that do.
5. To wear no *needless ornaments,* such as rings, earrings, necklaces, lace, or ruffles.
6. *To use no needless self-indulgence.*

II. Zealously to maintain good works; in particular,

1. To *give alms* of such things as you possess, and that according to your ability.
2. To reprove those who sin in your sight, and that in love and meekness of wisdom.
3. To be patterns of *diligence* and *frugality,* of *self-denial,* and taking up the cross daily.

III. Constantly to attend on all the ordinances of God; in particular,

1. To be at church, and at the Lord's table, and at every public meeting of the Bands, at every opportunity.

2. To use private prayer every day; and family prayer, if you are the head of a family.

3. Frequently to read the Scriptures, and meditate thereon. And,

4. To observe as days of fasting or abstinence all *Fridays* in the year.

Section III.

OF CLASS MEETINGS.

Ques. 1. How may the Leaders of Classes be rendered more useful?

Ans. 1. Let each of them be diligently examined concerning his method of meeting a Class. Let this be done with all possible exactness, at least once a quarter. In order to this take sufficient time.

2. Let each Leader carefully inquire how every soul in his Class prospers: not only how each person observes the outward rules, but how he grows in the knowledge and love of God.

3. Let the Leaders converse frequently and freely with those who have the charge of their Circuits.

Ques. 2. Can anything more be done in order to make the Class Meetings lively and profitable?

Ans. 1. Change improper Leaders.

2. Let the Leaders frequently meet each other's Classes.

3. Let us observe which Leaders are the most useful; and let these meet the other Classes as often as possible.

4. See that all the Leaders be not only men of sound judgment, but men truly devoted to God.

5. As a general rule let no Leader have charge of more than one Class.

Ques. 3. How shall we prevent improper persons from insinuating themselves into the Church ?

Ans. 1. *Give Tickets to none until they are recommended by a Leader, with whom they have met at least three months on trial.*

2. Give trial tickets to none but those who are recommended by one you know, or until they have met three or four times in a Class.

3. Read the rules to them the first time they meet.

4. Private members in connection with other Evangelical Churches, or with any seceding body of Methodists, who make application for admission into our Church, may be received by the Ministers on the Circuit as members without the usual term of probation.

Ques. 4. What shall we do with those members of our Church who wilfully and repeatedly neglect to meet in Class ?

Ans. 1. Let the Chairman, or one of the Preachers, visit them whenever it is practicable, and explain to them the consequence if they continue to neglect, viz., exclusion.

2. If they do not amend, let him who has the charge of the Circuit exclude them, (in the church), showing that they are laid aside for a breach of our rules of Discipline, and not for immoral conduct.

Ques. 5. How often shall we permit those who are not of our Church to be present at our Class Meetings and Lovefeasts ?

Ans. Let them be admitted with the utmost caution, and, to the Love-feast, not without a note of admittance.

Section IV.

OF MARRIAGE.

Ques. 1. Do we observe any evil which has prevailed in our Church with respect to marriage?

Ans. Many of our members have married with *unawakened* persons. This has produced bad effects: they have been either hindered for life, or have turned back to perdition.

Ques. 2. What can be done to discourage this?

Ans. 1. Let every Minister or Preacher publicly enforce the Apostle's caution, "Be ye not unequally yoked together with unbelievers."—2 Cor. vi. 14.

2. Let him declare, whoever does this will be put back on trial for three months.

3. When any such is put back on trial, let a suitable exhortation be subjoined.

4. Let all be exhorted to take no steps in so weighty a matter, without advising with the most serious of their brethren.

Ques. 3. Ought any woman to marry without the consent of her parents?

Ans. In general she ought not. Yet there may be exceptions. For if, 1st. A woman believe it to be her duty to marry; if, 2nd. Her parents absolutely refuse to let her marry any Christian, then she may, nay, ought to, marry without their consent. Yet even then, a Methodist Preacher ought not to be married to her.

We do not prevent our people from marrying persons who are not of our Church, provided such persons have the form and are seeking the power of godliness; but we are determined to discourage their marrying persons who do not come up to this description. And even in a doubtful case, the member shall be put back on trial.

Section V.

OF DRESS.

Ques. Should we insist on the rules concerning dress?

Ans. By all means. This is no time to give any encouragement to superfluity of apparel; therefore, give no tickets to any till they have left off superfluous ornaments. In order to this, 1. Let every one who has the charge of a circuit read the thoughts upon dress, at least once a year, in every large society. 2. In visiting the classes, be very mild, but very strict. 3. Allow of no exempt case:—Better one suffer than many. 4. Give no tickets to any, who, in their mode of dress, exceed the plainness and moderation enjoined in the New Testament.

CHAPTER V.

OF BRINGING MINISTERS AND MEMBERS TO TRIAL, AND OF INSOLVENCIES AND THE SETTLEMENT OF DISPUTES.

Section I.

OF THE TRIAL OF MINISTERS AND TRAVELLING PREACHERS.

Ques. 1. What shall be done when a Minister or Preacher is under report of being guilty of some crime expressly forbidden in the word of God, as an unchristian practice, sufficient to exclude a person from the kingdom of grace and glory?

Ans. 1. If the accused be the President of the Conference, the Co-Delegate—or in his absence the Chairman of the District on which the President resides—is required to select a Committee of at least five Ministers to investigate the case, and shall preside at the trial.

2. The presiding officer shall furnish the accused, in due time, with an exact copy of the charge, or charges, and specifications in writing, and the time and place of trial.

3. If the accused be the Co-Delegate, a Missionary Secre-

tary, or a Chairman of a District, the President of Conference—or in his absence a Deputy appointed by him, who shall be a Chairman of a District—shall select the Committee to investigate the case, and shall preside at the trial.

4. If the accused be a Minister, or a Travelling Preacher, then,—

1. Let the Chairman, in the absence of the President, call as many Ministers as he shall think fit—at least three —and if possible bring the accused and the accuser face to face.

2. If the person be clearly convicted, he shall be admonished, reproved, suspended, or dealt with as the Committee may judge expedient, until the next ensuing District Meeting.

3. If the accuser and the accused cannot be brought face to face, but the alleged delinquent evades trial, it shall be received as presumptive proof of guilt, and out of the mouth of two or three witnesses he shall be condemned. Nevertheless, in that case, as well as in all others, the District Meeting shall examine into it; shall dispose of the case as it judges expedient; and shall report to the Conference, where the whole matter shall be finally determined.

4. If a Minister or Preacher be charged with immorality between the time of holding the District Meeting and the Conference, a Committee chosen as above directed shall investigate the matter, and shall have authority to admonish, reprove, or suspend the offender until the Conference, when the case shall be finally determined.

5. If there be a difference between any of the Ministers or Preachers, the respective parties shall choose two Ministers; and the Chairman of the District on which the respondent resides, with the four Ministers so chosen, shall be the final arbitrators to determine the matter in dispute.

6. In case of dispute between a Minister or Preacher and any one of our members, relative to matters of secular business, the Chairman of the District shall recommend an arbitration, over which he shall preside, consisting of a Minister or lay member of our Church, chosen by each of the parties; which two persons thus chosen shall call a third member or Minister, to whom the matter shall be referred. In case of the failure of this arbitration to satisfy either of the parties, the dissatisfied party may proceed against the other before our regular Church courts.

7. If any Minister or Preacher shall have contracted debts which he is not able to pay, let the Chairman appoint three judicious Ministers to be a Committee of inquiry into the circumstances of the supposed delinquent, and if, in their opinion, he has acted dishonestly, or contracted debts without a probability of paying, let him be reproved, suspended, or disposed of as the Committee may judge expedient, until the next ensuing District Meeting.

8. In every case of equality the Chairman shall have a casting vote.

Ques. 2. What shall be done in cases of improper tempers, words, or actions?

Ans. The person so offending shall be reproved by his senior in office. Should a second transgression take place, one or more Ministers or Preachers shall be taken as witnesses. If he be not then cured, he shall be tried at the next District Meeting.

Ques. 3. What shall be done with those Ministers or Preachers who may hold, and disseminate publicly or privately, doctrines which are contrary to our Articles of Religion?

Ans. Let the same process be observed as in cases of gross immorality; but if the Minister or Preacher so offending do solemnly engage not to disseminate such erroneous doctrines, in public or in private, he shall be borne with until his case be laid before the next Conference, which shall determine the matter.

Ques. 4. What shall be done in case any Minister or Travelling Preacher follow a trade, or be engaged in any secular business?

Ans. If any Travelling Minister, Preacher, or Missionary be employed in, or carry on any trade, he shall, on proof thereof, be excluded from the Itinerant Plan; as we judge such pursuit of private emolument is incompatible with our Ministerial duties. No Minister or Preacher who will not relinquish his trade of *buying and selling*, though it were only pills, drops, or balsams, shall be considered a Minister or Travelling Preacher any longer. Selling *our own* books is an exception.

Section II.

OF THE TRIAL OF LOCAL PREACHERS.

1. When charges are preferred against a Local Preacher, the accused and the accuser shall respectively choose two Local Preachers, or other official members on the circuit; or, in the event of either or both parties refusing to make the necessary choice, the Superintendent shall name such persons as he may deem proper, being official members, to constitute the Committee, and shall, with the said Committee, try the accused preacher, and they shall have authority, if he be found guilty, to admonish, reprove, or suspend him, till the ensuing Local Preachers' Meeting, or Quarterly Official Meeting, when the whole matter shall be determined.

2. The Superintendent shall, on receiving a complaint against a Local Preacher, send a copy of the charge, or charges, and specifications, to the person accused, with the name of the accuser or accusers, before he calls a Committee to examine into the charge; and shall have a casting vote in case of equality.

Ques. What shall be done in cases of improper tempers, words, or actions?

Ans. The person so offending shall be reprehended by the Superintendent. Should a second transgression take place, one or more faithful friends shall be taken as witnesses. If he be not cured, he shall be tried at the next Local Preachers' Meeting, or Quarterly Official Meeting of the Circuit, and if found guilty and impenitent he shall be expelled from the Church.

Ques. 2. What shall be done when a Local Preacher fails in business, or contracts debts which he is not able to pay?

Ans. 1. The Superintendent Minister shall appoint three judicious members of the Church to inspect the accounts, contracts, and circumstances of the supposed delinquent; and if, in their opinion, he has behaved dishonestly, or contracted debts without the probability of paying, he shall be suspended until the ensuing Local Preachers' Meeting, or Quarterly Official Meeting, which shall examine into, and determine the case.

2. In every case, a Local Preacher under censure, or suspension by the Local Preachers' Meeting, or the Quarterly Official Meeting, shall have the right of appeal to the ensuing District Meeting, by giving notice of his intention to do so at the time of such suspension.

Section III.

OF THE TRIAL OF MEMBERS OF THE CHURCH.

Ques. How shall an accused member be brought to trial?

Ans. 1. Before the Society of which he is a member, or a select number of them, in the presence of the President, Chairman, Minister or Preacher, in the following manner:—Let the accused and the accuser be brought face to face; but if this cannot be done, let the next best evidence be procured. If the accused person be found guilty, by a decision of a majority of the members before whom he is brought to trial, and the crime be such as is expressly forbidden by the Word of God, sufficient to exclude a person from the kingdom of grace and glory, let the Minister or Preacher who has the charge of the Circuit expel him. If the accused person evade a trial, by absenting himself, after sufficient notice given him, and the circumstances of the accusation be strong and presumptive, let him be esteemed as guilty, and accordingly excluded. Witnesses from without shall not be rejected.

2. But in case of neglect of duties of any kind, imprudent conduct, indulging sinful tempers or words, or disobedience to the order and discipline of the Church:—First, let private reproof be given by a Minister, Preacher or Leader. On a second offence, the Minister, Preacher or Leader, may take one or two faithful friends, and if there be acknowledgment of the fault and proper humiliation, we will bear with him for a season. On a third offence let the case be brought before the Society, or a select number, and if there be no sign of real humiliation, the offender must be cut off.

3. If a member of our Church shall be tried and convicted of endeavouring to sow dissensions in any of our Societies, by inveighing against either our Doctrines or Discipline, such person so offending shall be first reproved by the Superintendent of his Circuit, and, if he persist in such pernicious practices, he shall be expelled from the Church.

4. Nevertheless, if, in any of the above-mentioned cases, the Superintendent differ in judgment from the majority of the Society, or the select number, concerning the innocence or guilt of the accused person, the trial, in such case, may be referred by the Minister or Preacher to the ensuing Quarterly Official Meeting.

5. If there be a murmur or complaint from an excluded person, in any of the above-mentioned instances, that justice has not been done, he shall be allowed an appeal to the *next* Quarterly Meeting : except such as absent themselves from trial, after sufficient notice is given them ;—and the majority of the Members of the Meeting present, shall finally determine the case.

6. In all cases of trial the Chairman of the Committee shall cause exact minutes to be taken and recorded of the charges, testimony, and examination, together with the decision of the Committee : which record, when read and approved, shall be signed by the Chairman, and also by the members of such Committee who are present, or a majority of them, and be preserved among the official documents of the Circuit.

7. On any dispute between two or more of the Members of our Church, concerning the payment of debts, or otherwise, which cannot be settled by the parties concerned, the Superintendent of the Circuit shall inquire into the circum-

stances of the case, and shall recommend to the contending parties a reference, consisting of one arbitrator chosen by the plaintiff, and another chosen by the defendant, which two arbitrators so chosen, shall nominate a third,—the three arbitrators being Members of our Church.

In all cases of arbitration, the report thereof shall be handed to the Superintendent of the Circuit.

8. But if one of the parties be dissatisfied with the judgment given, such party may apply to the ensuing Quarterly Official Meeting of the Circuit for permission to have a *second* arbitration appointed; and if the Meeting see sufficient reason, they shall grant a *second* arbitration, in which case each party shall choose two arbitrators, and the four arbitrators shall choose a fifth, the judgment of the majority of whom shall be final; and any person refusing to abide by it shall be be excluded from the Church.

9. And if any Member of our Church shall refuse, in case of debt or other disputes, to refer the matter to arbitration, when recommended by the Superintendent of the Circuit, or shall enter into a law-suit with another Member before these measures are taken, he shall be expelled, unless the case be of such a nature as to require and justify a process at law.

10. The Superintendents of Circuits are required to execute all our rules fully and strenuously against all frauds, and particularly against dishonest insolvencies, suffering none to remain in the Church on any account, who are found guilty of any fraud.

11. To prevent scandal, when any of our Members fail in business, or contract debts which they are not able to pay, let two or three judicious Members of the Church inspect the accounts of the supposed delinquent; and if he has

behaved dishonestly, or borrowed money without a probability of paying, let him be expelled.

12. Whenever a complaint is made against a Member of the Church, for non-payment of debt—when the accounts are adjusted and the amount ascertained—the Superintendent shall call the debtor before a Committee of at least three, to show cause why he does not make payment. The Committee shall determine what further time shall be granted him for payment, and what security, if any, shall be given for payment; and in case the debtor refuses to comply, he shall be expelled; but in such case he may appeal to the Quarterly Official Meeting, and their decision shall be final. And in case the creditor complains that justice is not done him, he may lay his grievance before the Quarterly Official Meeting, and their decision shall be final; and if the creditor refuses to comply, he shall be expelled.

13. After such form of trial and expulsion, such persons shall have no privileges of Society, or Sacraments in our Church, without contrition, confession, and proper trial.

14. In all judicial proceedings, arbitrations, or committees of inquiry, involving the standing, or Church relation, of any of our Ministers or members, the President, or a Chairman of a District, or a Minister, or Preacher shall preside.

CHAPTER VI.

TEMPORAL ECONOMY.

Section I.

OF THE BOUNDARIES OF THE CONFERENCE, &c.

There shall be one Conference in Canada, which shall meet once a year.

Ques. 1. How are the Districts to be formed?

Ans. According to the judgment of the President and Stationing Committee.

Ques. 2. How are Circuits and Missions to be formed?

Ans. By the Stationing Committee, on the recommmendation of the District Meeting: provided nevertheless, that circuits supporting their own ministers or preachers shall not be divided till such divisions have been approved of by their respective Quarterly Meetings, and their approval signified in writing by the Recording Steward; or, otherwise, by a *two-thirds* vote of the Annual District Meeting, when the Stewards are present.

3. On the Division of a Circuit, no minister who has travelled successively the three preceding years on such Circuit shall be appointed to either part of it—nevertheless,

this rule shall not apply to those places which may be transferred in adjusting the work by the District Meeting, which transfer has been sanctioned by the Stationing Committee.

Section II.

OF THE SALARIES OF MINISTERS AND PREACHERS, AND THE ALLOWANCES TO THEIR WIVES, WIDOWS, AND CHILDREN.

1. The salary of a married Minister shall be $240 per annum, and his travelling expenses.

2. The salary of a Preacher on trial shall be $140, and his travelling expenses.

3. A Minister's salary after he is received into full connexion and ordained, shall be $180 per annum, while he remains single.

4. No reduction shall be made in a Minister's salary during the year, in the event of the death of his wife.

5. Each child of a Travelling Minister, born after the father was received into full connexion with the Conference and ordained, shall be allowed $30 per annum until 18 years of age—if not otherwise provided for.

6. The children of Superannuated Ministers shall receive from the Children's Fund according to the provisions of that fund.

Scale of Allowances to Superannuated Ministers, and the Widows of Ministers who have died in the Work.

1. Every Superannuated Minister who has travelled effectively fifteen years, shall receive $128 per annum, and from fifteen years and upwards shall receive $8 per annum for each year of effective service.

2. Every Superannuated Minister who has travelled eleven years, and less than fifteen years, shall receive $128 per annum for four years.

3. Every Superannuated Minister who has travelled eight years, and less than eleven years, shall receive $80 per annum for four years.

4. Any Minister who may locate and enter into secular business, and subsequently be received into the Conference, shall not be allowed any claim for services during his first period of labour.

5. It shall be competent for the Board, upon the recommendation of the Conference, to commute with such Ministers as may become Superannuated from causes which do not disqualify them for active business, by paying them such sums as may be deemed equitable, instead of allowing them to become permanent claimants upon the Superannuated Ministers' Fund.

6. Ministers who retire temporarily from the work, on account of ill health or accident, while they receive from the Superannuated Ministers' Fund, according to their years of service, shall not be precluded from receiving aid, to such amount as the Conference may recommend, from the Contingent or Missionary Fund, as they may have been engaged in regular or mission work.

7. The widows of deceased Ministers shall be allowed two-thirds of the amount appropriated to their husbands, according to the foregoing scale, except such widows as were ten years younger than their husbands, and were married after their husbands were fifty-five years of age, or after they were superannuated. These shall have no claims except by the recommendation of the Board, and at the entire discretion of the Conference.

Provided always, that when the claims upon the Superannuated Ministers' Fund for any year shall be more than the income of such year, each claimant shall receive a per centage in proportion to his or her claims, to the full amount only of the current income.

8. Any Minister who shall be expelled from the Conference, or shall hereafter leave the effective work for other employment, or to labour in other countries, shall thereby forfeit to the Superannuated Ministers' Fund the amount which he may have paid into it.

Section III.

OF THE QUALIFICATIONS, APPOINTMENT, AND DUTIES OF THE STEWARDS OF CIRCUITS.

Ques. 1. What are the qualifications necessary for Stewards?

Ans. Let them be men of solid piety, who both know and love the Methodist doctrine and discipline, and of good natural and acquired abilities to transact the temporal business.

Ques. 2. How are Stewards to be appointed?

Ans. They shall be appointed by the vote of the November Quarterly Official Meeting, the Superintendent nominating.

Ques. 3. What are the duties of Stewards?

Ans. To take an exact account of whatever has been collected for the support of Ministers and Preachers in the Circuit; to make an accurate return of every expenditure

QUALIFICATIONS OF STEWARDS. 87

of money, whether to the Minister, the Preacher, the sick or the poor; to seek the needy and distressed, in order to relieve and comfort them; to inform the Ministers or Preachers of any sick or disorderly persons; to attend the Quarterly Meetings of their Circuits; to give advice, if asked, in planning the Circuit; to provide the elements for the Lord's Supper; to write circular letters to the Societies in the Circuit to be more liberal if need be; to let them know, when occasion requires, the state of the temporal concerns at the last Quarterly Meeting; to fill up the Circuit schedules correctly; and to be subject to the President, the Chairman of their District, and the Ministers and Preachers of their Circuit.

Ques. 4. To whom are the Stewards accountable for the faithful performance of their duties?

Ans. To the Quarterly Official Meeting of the Circuit.

Ques. 5. What number of Stewards is necessary in each Circuit?

Ans. 1. Not less than three, nor more than seven; one of whom shall be the Recording Steward, who shall be nominated by the Superintendent, and approved by the meeting.

2. When a Recording Steward of a Circuit becomes incapacitated for the duties of his office, the Superintendent of the Circuit shall have authority to appoint another of the Stewards to that office until the next Quarterly Meeting, when his place shall be supplied according to discipline.

Section IV.
OF THE BUILDING OF CHURCHES AND PARSONAGES, AND THE ORDER TO BE OBSERVED THEREIN.

Ques. 1. Is anything advisable in regard to building?

Ans. 1. Let our churches be built plain and decent, and not more expensive than is absolutely necessary.

2. In order more effectually to prevent our people from contracting debts which they are not able to discharge, it shall be the duty of the Quarterly Official Meeting of every Circuit, where it is contemplated to build a church or churches, to secure the ground or lot on which such church or churches are to be built, according to our deed of settlement, which deed must be legally executed; and also, said Quarterly Meeting shall appoint a judicious Committee of at least three members of our Church, who shall form an estimate of the amount necessary to build; and three-fourths of the money, according to such estimate, shall be secured or subscribed before any such building shall be commenced. All church property to be legally secured, and the deed registered within one year after its execution.

3. In future, we will admit no charter, deed, or conveyance, for any church to be used by us, unless it be provided in such charter, deed, or conveyance, that the Trustees of the said church shall, at all times, permit such Ministers and Preachers belonging to the Wesleyan Methodist Church, as shall from time to time be duly authorised by the Conference or by the Ministers of our Church, to preach and expound God's Holy Word, and to execute the Discipline of the Church, and to administer the Sacraments therein, according to the true meaning and purport of our deed of settlement.

4. When a new Board of Trustees is to be created, it shall be done by the appointment of the Quarterly Official Meeting, upon the nomination of the Superintendent of the Circuit, and shall consist of not less than seven nor more than twenty-one.

5. No person shall be eligible as a Trustee to any of our churches, parsonages, school-houses, burial-grounds, or other property, who is not a member of our Church.

6. No person who is a Trustee, shall be ejected while he is in joint security for money, unless such relief be given him as is demanded, or as the creditor will accept.

7. When and so often as one or more of the said Trustees, or of their successors in the said trust, shall die, withdraw, or cease to be a member or members of the said Wesleyan Methodist Church, according to the Rules and Discipline of the said Church, the vacant place of the Trustee or Trustees so dying, withdrawing, or ceasing to be a member or members of the said Church, shall be filled with a successor or successors, being a member or members of the said Church, of the full age of twenty-one years, to be nominated and appointed as follows: that is to say,— to be nominated by the Wesleyan Methodist Minister having charge for the time being of the Circuit in which the said premises shall be situate, and thereupon appointed by the surviving or remaining Trustee or Trustees of the said trust, or a majority of them, if he or they shall think proper to appoint the person or persons so nominated, and, in case of an equal division of the votes of the Trustees present, at any meeting of the Trustees held for the purpose of such appointment, the Minister in charge of the said Circuit shall have a casting vote in such appointment; and if it shall happen at any time that there shall be no sur-

viving or remaining Trustee of the said trust, in every such case it shall and may be lawful for the Minister aforesaid to nominate, and the Quarterly Official Meeting of the Circuit, if they approve of the persons so nominated, to appoint the requisite number of Trustees, the said Trustees of the said trust, by a vote of the majority of the members of the said meeting then present, and in case of an equal division of their votes, the Chairman of the said meeting shall have the casting vote in such appointment, and the person or persons so nominated and appointed Trustee or Trustees in either of the said modes of nomination and appointment, shall be the legal successor or successors of the said above named Trustees, and shall have in perpetual succession the same capacities, powers, rights and duties, as belonged to and were exercised by the original Trustees.

Ques. 2. What other directions are necessary with regard to church property?

Ans. 1. In order to prevent forgetfulness and loss of Church property, a correct inventory of all our property, whether Lands, Churches, Parsonages, or Furniture, shall be kept.

2. The Book Steward for the time being shall be the Registrar, and shall provide and keep a proper Book for the purpose, which book shall be laid before the Conference, for the inspection of its members.

3. Each Superintendent shall return a list and description of Church property within the circumference of his Circuit, every fourth year, according to Conference schedule, and at the time of the valuation of the Book Room property; also the exact locality and other information needful; and whether, and where, the Deeds are registered.

Ques. 3. What advice or direction shall be given concerning the building or renting of dwelling houses for the use of the Travelling Ministers?

Ans. 1. It is recommended by the Conference that Parsonages be obtained on each of our Circuits and Missions wherever practicable, for the use of our married Ministers and their families; and be secured according to our deed of settlement: or, where this is impracticable, that suitable houses be rented.

3. It shall be the duty of the Chairmen and Ministers to use their influence to carry the above rules, respecting building and renting houses for the Ministers and their families, into effect. In order to this, each Quarterly Official Meeting shall appoint a Committee (unless other measures have been adopted) who, with the advice and aid of the Ministers and Chairman, shall devise such means as may seem fit to raise monies for that purpose. And the Conference shall make special inquiry of their members respecting this part of their duty.

CHAPTER VII.

SACRAMENTAL AND OTHER SERVICES.

In the Administration of the Ordinances, let the following forms be used.

SECTION I.

THE MINISTRATION OF BAPTISM TO INFANTS.

The Minister coming to the font, which is to be filled with pure water, shall use the following, or some other exhortation, suitable to this sacred office.

Dearly beloved, forasmuch as all men are conceived and born in sin, and that our Saviour Christ saith, None can enter into the kingdom of God, except he be regenerate and born anew of water and of the Holy Ghost; I beseech you to call upon God the Father, through our Lord Jesus Christ, that having of his bounteous mercy redeemed [*this child*] by the blood of his Son, He will grant that [*he*] being baptized with water may also be baptized with the Holy Ghost, received into Christ's holy Church, and become [*a lively member*] of the same.

SACRAMENTAL SERVICES—BAPTISM OF INFANTS.

Then shall the Minister say,—Let us Pray.

Almighty and everlasting God, who of thy great mercy didst save Noah and his family in the ark from perishing by water; and also didst safely lead the children of Israel, thy people, through the Red Sea, figuring thereby thy holy baptism, and hast set apart water for this Holy Sacrament; and who hast condescended to enter into gracious covenant with man, wherein thou hast included children as partakers of its benefits, declaring that, "of such is the kingdom of heaven;" we beseech thee, for thine infinite mercies, that thou wilt look upon [*this child*]; wash [*him*] and sanctify [*him*] with the Holy Ghost; that [*he,*] having been delivered from thy wrath, may be received into the ark of Christ's Church, and being steadfast in faith, joyful through hope, and rooted in love, may so pass the waves of this troublesome world, that finally [*he*] may come to the land of everlasting life; there to reign with thee, world without end, through Jesus Christ our Lord. *Amen.*

O merciful God, grant that the old Adam in [*this child*] may be so buried, that the new man may be raised up in [*him.*] *Amen.*

Grant that all carnal affections may die in [*him,*] and that all things belonging to the Spirit may live and grow in [*him*]. *Amen.*

Grant that [*he*] may have power and strength to have victory, and to triumph against the devil, the world, and the flesh. *Amen.*

Grant that whosoever is dedicated to thee by our office and Ministry, may also be endued with heavenly virtues, and everlastingly rewarded through thy mercy, O blessed Lord God, who dost live and govern all things, world without end   *Amen.*

Almighty, ever living God, whose most dearly beloved Son Jesus Christ, for the forgiveness of our sins, did shed out of his most precious side both water and blood, and gave commandment to his Disciples that they should go teach all nations, and baptize them in the name of the Father, and of the Son, and of the Holy Ghost; Regard, we beseech thee, the supplications of this congregation; and grant that [*this child,*] now to be baptized, may receive the fulness of thy grace, and be found at last in the number of thy faithful and elect children, through Jesus Christ our Lord. *Amen.*

Then shall the people stand up: and the Minister shall say,—
Hear the words of the Gospel, written by St. Mark, in the tenth chapter, beginning at the thirteenth verse :—

They brought young children to Christ, that he should touch them. And his Disciples rebuked those that brought them. But when Jesus saw it he was much displeased, and said unto them, Suffer the little children to come unto me, and forbid them not, for of such is the kingdom of God. Verily I say unto you, Whosoever shall not receive the kingdom of God as a little child, he shall not enter therein. And he took them in his arms, put his hands upon them, and blessed them.

Then the Minister shall take the child in his arms, and say to the Parents or Friends of the Child, "Name the Child," and then, naming it after them, he shall Baptize the Child, saying,

N. I Baptize thee in the name of the Father, and of the Son, and of the Holy Ghost. *Amen.*

Then shall be said, all kneeling,

Our Father, who art in heaven, Hallowed be thy name.

Thy kingdom come. Thy will be done on earth as it is in heaven. Give us this day our daily bread. And forgive us our trespasses, as we forgive them that trespass against us. And lead us not into temptation, but deliver us from evil. Amen.

Then the Minister may conclude with extempore prayer.

Section II.

THE MINISTRATION OF BAPTISM TO ADULTS.

The Minister shall use the following, or some other exhortation suitable to this holy office.

Dearly beloved, forasmuch as all men are conceived and born in sin, (and that which is born of the flesh is flesh, and they that are in the flesh cannot please God, but live in sin,-committing many actual transgressions;) and our Saviour Christ saith, None can enter into the kingdom of God, except he be regenerate and born anew of water and of the Holy Ghost; I beseech you to call upon God the Father, through our Lord Jesus Christ, that, of his bounteous goodness he will grant to [*these persons,*] that which by nature [*they*] cannot have; that [*they*] may be baptised, not only with water but also with the Holy Ghost, and received into Christ's holy Church, and be made lively [*members*] of the same.

Then shall the Minister say,

Almighty and immortal God, the aid of all that need, the helper of all that flee to thee for succour, the life of them that believe, and the resurrection of the dead; We call upon thee for [*these persons;*] that [*they,*] coming to thy holy baptism, may be filled with the Holy Ghost. Receive [*them,*] O Lord, as thou hast promised by thy well-beloved Son, saying,—Ask and ye shall receive,—seek and ye shall find,—knock and it shall be opened unto you: So give now unto us that ask; let us that seek find; open the gate unto us that knock; that [*these persons*] may enjoy the everlasting benediction of thy heavenly washing, and may come to the eternal kingdom which thou hast promised by Christ our Lord. *Amen.*

After which he shall say,

Almighty and everlasting God, heavenly Father, we give thee humble thanks for that thou hast vouchsafed to call us to the knowledge of thy grace and faith in thee; increase this knowledge and confirm this faith in us evermore. Give thy Holy Spirit to [*these persons,*] that [*they*] may be made [*heirs*] of everlasting salvation, through our Lord Jesus Christ, who liveth and reigneth with thee and the Holy Spirit, now and forever. *Amen.*

O merciful God, grant that the old Adam in [*these persons*] may be so buried that the new man may be raised up in [*them.*] *Amen.*

Grant that all carnal affections may die in [*them,*] and that all things belonging to the Spirit may live and grow in [*them.*] *Amen.*

Grant that [*they*] may have power and strength to have victory, and to triumph against the devil, the world, and the flesh. *Amen.*

Grant that [*they,*] being here dedicated to thee by our office and Ministry, may also be endued with heavenly virtues, and everlastingly rewarded through thy mercy, O blessed Lord God, who dost live and govern all things, world without end. *Amen.*

Almighty, ever living God, whose most dearly beloved Son, Jesus Christ, for the forgiveness of our sins, did shed out of his most precious side both water and blood, and gave commandment to his disciples that they should go teach all nations, and baptise them in the name of the Father, and of the Son, and of the Holy Ghost; Regard, we beseech thee, the supplications of this congregation, and grant that [*these persons*] now to be baptised may receive the fulness of thy grace, and be found, at last, in the number of thy faithful and elect children, through Jesus Christ our Lord. *Amen.*

Then shall the people stand up, and the Minister shall say,—Hear the words of the Gospel, written by St. John, in the third chapter, beginning at the first verse:

There was a man of the Pharisees, named Nicodemus, a ruler of the Jews; the same came to Jesus by night, and said unto him, Rabbi, we know that thou art a teacher come from God; for no man can do these miracles that thou doest, except God be with him. Jesus answered and said unto him, Verily, verily, I say unto thee, Except a man be born again, he cannot see the kingdom of God. Nicodemus saith unto him, How can a man be born when he is old? Can he enter the second time into his mother's womb, and be born? Jesus answered, Verily, verily, I say unto thee, Except a man be born of water and of the Spirit, he cannot enter into the kingdom of God. That which is born of the flesh is flesh, and that which is born of the Spirit is spirit. Marvel not that I said unto thee, Ye must be born again. The wind bloweth where it listeth, and thou hearest the sound thereof; but canst not tell whence it cometh and whither it goeth; so is every one that is born of the Spirit.

Then the Minister shall speak to the Persons to be Baptised on this wise:

Well-beloved, who [*have*] come hither, desiring to receive holy baptism, [*ye*] have heard how the congregation have prayed that our Lord Jesus Christ would vouchsafe to receive you, and bless you, to release you of your sins, to give you the kingdom of heaven and everlasting life. And our Lord Jesus Christ hath promised, in his Holy Word, to grant all those things that we have prayed for; which promise he for his part will most assuredly keep and perform.

Wherefore, after this promise made by Christ, you must also faithfully, for your part, promise, in the presence of this whole congregation, that you will renounce the devil and all his works, and constantly believe God's Holy Word, and obediently keep his Commandments.

Then shall the Minister demand of each of the Persons to be Baptised, severally:

Ques. Dost thou renounce the devil and all his works, the vain pomp and glory of the world, with all covetous desires of the same, and the carnal desires of the flesh, so that thou wilt not follow or be led by them?

Ans. I renounce them all.

Ques. Dost thou believe in God the Father Almighty, Maker of heaven and earth? and in Jesus Christ his only begotten Son our Lord? and that he was conceived by the Holy Ghost, born of the Virgin Mary? that He suffered under Pontius Pilate, was crucified, dead, and buried? that he arose again the third day? that he ascended into heaven, and sitteth at the right hand of God the Father Almighty, and from thence he shall come again, at the end of the world, to judge the quick and the dead?

And dost thou believe in the Holy Ghost; the Holy Catholic Church; the Communion of Saints; the Remission of Sins; the Resurrection of the Body, and Everlasting Life after death?

Ans. All this I steadfastly believe.

Ques. Wilt thou be baptised in this faith?

Ans. That is my desire.

Ques. Wilt thou then obediently keep God's holy will and commandments, and walk in the same all the days of thy life?

Ans. I will endeavour so to do, God being my helper.

Then shall the Minister ask the name of the person to be baptised, and repeating the name shall baptise him, saying:

N, I Baptise thee in the name of the Father, and of the Son, and of the Holy Ghost. *Amen.*

Then shall be said the Lord's Prayer, all kneeling.

Our Father who art in heaven, Hallowed be thy name. Thy kingdom come. Thy will be done on earth, as it is in heaven. Give us this day our daily bread. And forgive us our trespasses, as we forgive them that trespass against us. And lead us not into temptation, but deliver us from evil. *Amen.*

The Minister may conclude with extempore prayer.

Section III.

OF THE LORD'S SUPPER.

THE ORDER FOR ADMINISTRATION OF THE LORD'S SUPPER.

While the Collection for the Poor is being taken up, the Minister shall say one or more of these sentences:

Let your light so shine before men that they may see your good works, and glorify your Father who is in heaven.— Matt. v. 16.

Lay not up for yourselves treasures upon earth, where moth and rust doth corrupt, and where thieves break through and steal; but lay up for yourselves treasures in heaven, where neither moth nor rust doth corrupt, and where thieves do not break through nor steal.—Matt. vi. 19, 20.

Whatsoever ye would that men should do unto you, even so do unto them: for this is the law and the prophets.— Matt. vii. 12.

Not every one that saith unto me, Lord, Lord, shall enter into the kingdom of heaven, but he that doeth the will of my Father who is in heaven.—Matt. vi. 21.

Zaccheus stood forth and said unto the Lord, Behold, Lord, the half of my goods I give to the poor; and if I have done any wrong to any man I restore him fourfold.—Luke xix. 8.

He that soweth sparingly shall reap also sparingly; and he that soweth bountifully shall reap also bountifully. Let every man do according as he is disposed in his heart; not grudgingly, or of necessity; for God loveth a cheerful giver.—2 Cor. ix. 6, 7.

As we have therefore opportunity let us do good unto all men, especially unto them who are of the household of faith.— Gal. vi. 10.

Godliness with contentment is great gain; for we brought nothing into this world, and it is certain we can carry nothing out.—1 Tim. vi. 6, 7.

Charge them that are rich in this world, that they be not highminded, nor trust in uncertain riches, but in the living God, who giveth us richly all things to enjoy; that they do good, that they be rich in good works, ready to distribute, willing to communicate; laying up in store for themselves a good foundation against the time to come, that they may lay hold on eternal life.—1 Tim. vi. 17, 18, 19.

For God *is* not unrighteous to forget your work and labour of love, which ye have shewed toward his name, in that ye have ministered to the saints, and do minister.—Heb. vi. 10.

But to do good and to communicate forget not; for with such sacrifices God is well pleased.—Heb. xiii. 16.

But whoso hath this world's good, and seeth his brother have need, and shutteth up his bowels *of compassion* from him, how dwelleth the love of God in him ?—1 John iii. 17.

He that hath pity upon the poor lendeth unto the Lord; and that which he hath given will he pay him again.—Prov. xix. 17.

Blessed *is* he that considereth the poor: the Lord will deliver him in time of trouble.—Psalm xli. 1.

While these sentences are being read, some fit person, appointed for that purpose, shall receive the alms for the poor; and then bring them to the Minister, who shall place them upon the table.

After which the Minister shall say:

Ye that do truly and earnestly repent of your sins, and are in love and charity with your neighbours, and intend to lead a new life, following the commandments of God, and walking from henceforth in His Holy ways.; draw near with faith and take this Holy Sacrament to your comfort; and make your humble confession to Almighty God, meekly kneeling upon your knees.

Then shall this general confession be made by the Minister, in the name of all those that are minded to receive the Holy Communion, both he and all the people kneeling humbly upon their knees, and saying:

Almighty God, Father of our Lord Jesus Christ, Maker of all things, Judge of all men: we acknowledge and bewail our manifold sins and wickedness, which we from time to time most grievously have committed, by thought, word, and deed, against thy Divine Majesty, provoking most justly thy wrath and indignation against us. We do earnestly repent and are heartily sorry for these our misdoings; the remembrance of them is grievous unto us. Have mercy upon us, have mercy upon us, most merciful Father, for thy Son, our Lord Jesus Christ's sake, forgive us all that is past; and grant that we may ever hereafter serve and please thee in newness of life, to the honour and glory of thy name, through Jesus Christ our Lord. *Amen.*

Then shall the Minister say:

O Almighty God, our heavenly Father, who of thy great mercy hast promised forgiveness of sins to all them that with hearty repentance and true faith turn unto thee; have mercy upon us; pardon and deliver us from all our sins, confirm and strengthen us in all goodness, and bring us to everlasting life, through Jesus Christ our Lord. *Amen.*

The Collect.

Almighty God, unto whom all hearts are open, all desires known, and from whom no secrets are hid; cleanse the thoughts of our hearts by the inspiration of thy Holy Spirit, that we may perfectly love thee, and worthily magnify thy Holy Name, through Christ our Lord. *Amen.*

Then shall the Minister say:

It is very meet, right, and our bounden duty, that we should at all times and in all places, give thanks unto thee, O Lord, Holy Father, Almighty, Everlasting God.

SACRAMENTAL SERVICES—THE LORD'S SUPPER. 103

Therefore, with angels and archangels, and with all the company of heaven, we laud and magnify thy glorious Name, evermore praising thee, and saying, Holy, holy, holy, Lord God of Hosts, heaven and earth are full of thy glory. Glory be to thee, O Lord most high. *Amen.*

We do not presume to come to this thy Table, O merciful Lord, trusting in our own righteousness, but in thy manifold and great mercies. We are not worthy so much as to gather up the crumbs under thy table. But thou art the same Lord, whose property is always to have mercy; Grant us, therefore, gracious Lord, so to eat the flesh of thy dear Son Jesus Christ, and to drink his blood, that our sinful souls and bodies may be made clean by his death, and washed through his most precious blood, and that we may evermore dwell in him, and he in us. *Amen.*

Then the Minister shall offer the Prayer of Consecration, as followeth:

Almighty God, our heavenly Father, who of thy tender mercy didst give thy only Son Jesus Christ to suffer death upon the cross for our redemption ; who made there (by his oblation of himself once offered) a full, perfect, and sufficient sacrifice, oblation and satisfaction for the sins of the whole world : and did institute, and in his holy Gospel command us to continue a perpetual memory of that his precious death, until his coming again : hear us, O merciful Father, we most humbly beseech thee, and grant that we, receiving these thy creatures of bread and wine, according to thy Son our Saviour Jesus Christ's holy institution, in remembrance of his death and passion, may be partakers of his most blessed

Body and Blood, who in the same night that he was betrayed, took bread; (1) and when he had given thanks he brake it (2) and gave it to his disciples, saying, Take eat; this (3) is my body which is given for you; Do this in remembrance of me. Likewise after supper he took (4) the cup; and when he had given thanks, he gave it to them, saying, Drink ye all of this; for this (5) is my blood of the New Testament, which is shed for you, and for many, for the remission of sins; this do ye, as often as ye drink it, in remembrance of me. *Amen.*

(1) *Here the Minister may take the plate of bread into his hand.*

(2) *And here may break the bread.*

(3) *And here may lay his hands upon all the bread.*

(4) *Here he may take the cup in his hand.*

(5) *And here may lay his hands upon all the vessels which contain the wine.*

Then shall the Minister first receive the communion in both kinds himself, and then proceed to deliver the same to other Ministers in like manner (if any be present), and after that to the people also, in order, into their uncovered hands. And when he delivereth the bread, he shall say:

The Body of our Lord Jesus Christ, which was given for *thee,* preserve *thy soul* and *body* unto everlasting life. Take and eat this in remembrance that Christ died for *thee,* and feed on him in *thy heart* by faith, with thanksgiving.

And the Minister that delivereth the cup shall say:

The blood of our Lord Jesus Christ, which was shed for *thee,* preserve *thy soul* and *body* unto everlasting life. Drink this in remembrance that Christ's blood was shed for *thee,* and be thankful.

SACRAMENTAL SERVICES—THE LORD'S SUPPER. 105

If the consecrated Bread or Wine be all spent before all have communicated, the Minister may consecrate more, by repeating the Prayer of Consecration.

When all have communicated, the Minister shall return to the Lord's Table, and place upon it what remaineth of the consecrated elements, covering the same with a fair linen cloth.

Then shall the Minister say the Lord's Prayer; the people repeating after him every petition.

Our Father who art in Heaven, Hallowed be thy name; Thy Kingdom come; Thy will be done on earth as it is in heaven; Give us this day our daily bread; And forgive us our trespasses, as we forgive them that trespass against us; And lead us not into temptation, but deliver us from evil; For thine is the Kingdom, and the Power, and the Glory, for ever and ever. *Amen.*

After which shall be said as followeth:

O Lord our heavenly Father, we thy humble servants desire thy Fatherly goodness mercifully to accept this our sacrifice of praise and thanksgiving; most humbly beseeching thee to grant that, by the merits and death of thy Son Jesus Christ, and through faith in his blood, we and thy whole church may obtain remission of our sins, and all other benefits of his passion. And here we offer and present unto thee, O Lord, ourselves, our souls and bodies, to be a reasonable, holy and lively sacrifice unto thee; humbly beseeching thee that all we who are partakers of this holy Communion, may be filled with thy grace and heavenly benediction. And although we be unworthy, through our manifold sins, to offer unto thee any sacrifice; yet we beseech thee to accept this our bounden duty and service; not weighing our merits but pardoning our offences, through Jesus Christ our Lord: by whom, and with whom, in the unity of the Holy Ghost, all honour and glory be unto thee, O Father Almighty, world without end. *Amen.*

Then shall be said:

Glory be to God on high, and on earth peace, good will towards men. We praise thee, we bless thee, we worship thee, we glorify thee, we give thanks to thee for thy great glory, O Lord God, heavenly King, God the Father Almighty.

O Lord, the only begotten Son Jesus Christ; O Lord God, Lamb of God, Son of the Father, that takest away the sins of the world, have mercy upon us. Thou that takest away the sins of the world, receive our prayer. Thou that sittest at the right hand of God the Father, have mercy upon us.

For thou only art holy, thou only art the Lord; thou only, O Christ, with the Holy Ghost, art most high in the Glory of God the Father. *Amen.*

Then the Minister, if he see it expedient, may offer an extempore Prayer; and afterwards shall let the people depart with this blessing:

May the peace of God, which passeth all understanding, keep your hearts and minds in the knowledge and love of God, and of his Son Jesus Christ our Lord; and the blessing of God Almighty, the Father, the Son, and the Holy Ghost be amongst you, and remain with you always. Amen.

N.B.—If the Minister be straitened for time, he may omit any part of the service, except the prayer of Consecration.

Section IV.

THE FORM AND MANNER OF ORDAINING MINISTERS.

[When the day appointed by the President is come, there shall be a Sermon, or exhortation, declaring the Duty and Office of such as come to be admitted Ministers: how necessary that order is in the Church of Christ, and also how the people ought to esteem them in their office.]

After which, one of the Ministers shall present unto the President all them that are to be ordained, and say:

I present unto you these persons present to be ordained Ministers.

Then their names being read aloud, the President shall say unto the People:

Brethren, these are they whom we purpose, God willing, this day to ordain Ministers. For, after due examination, we find not to the contrary, but that they are lawfully called to this function and ministry, and that they are persons meet for the same. But if there be any of you who knoweth any impediment or crime in any of them, for the which he ought not to be received in this holy Ministry, let him come forth in the name of God, and show what the crime or impediment is.

[If any crime or impediment be objected, the President shall surcease from ordaining that person until such time as the party accused shall be found clear of the crime.]

Then shall be said the Collect, Epistle, and Gospel, as followeth.
The Collect.

Almighty God, giver of all good things, who by the Holy Spirit hast appointed Ministers in thy Church; mercifully behold these thy servants now called to the office of Ministers, and replenish them so with the truth of thy doctrine, and adorn them with innocency of life, that, both by word and good example, they may faithfully serve thee in this office, to the glory of thy name, and the edification of thy Church, through the merits of our Saviour Jesus Christ, who liveth and reigneth with thee and the Holy Ghost, world without end. *Amen.*

The Epistle. Eph. iv. 7-13.

Unto every one of us is given grace according to the measure of the gift of Christ. Wherefore he saith, when he ascended up on high he led captivity captive, and gave gifts unto men. (Now that he ascended, what is it but that he also descended first into the lower parts of the earth? He that descended is the same also that ascended up far above all heavens, that he might fill all things.) And he gave some Apostles; and some Prophets; and some Evangelists; and some Pastors and teachers; for the perfecting of the Saints, for the work of the Ministry, for the edifying of the body of Christ, till we all come in the unity of the faith, and of the knowledge of the Son of God, unto a perfect man, unto the measure of the stature of the fullness of Christ.

[*After this shall be read for the Gospel, part of the tenth chapter of St. John.*]

St. John x. 1-16.

Verily, verily, I say unto you, he that entereth not by the door into the sheepfold, but climbeth up some other way, the same is a thief and a robber. But he that entereth in by the door is the shepherd of the sheep. To him the porter openeth, and the sheep hear his voice, and he calleth his own sheep by name and leadeth them out. And when he putteth forth his own sheep he goeth before them, and the sheep follow him, for they know his voice. And a stranger will they not follow, but will flee from him: for they know not the voice of strangers. This parable spake Jesus unto them, but they understood not what things they were which he spake unto them. Then said Jesus unto them again, Verily, verily, I say unto you, I am the door of the sheep. All that ever came before me are thieves and robbers, but the sheep did not hear them. I am the door; by me if any man enter in he shall be saved, and shall go in and out, and find pasture. The thief cometh not but for to steal, and to kill, and to destroy; I am come that they might have life, and that they might have it more abundantly. I am the good shepherd: the good shepherd giveth his life for the sheep. But he that is an hireling, and not the shepherd, whose own the sheep are not, seeth the wolf coming, and leaveth the sheep, and fleeth, and the wolf catcheth them, and scattereth the sheep. The hireling fleeth because he is an hireling, and careth not for the sheep. I am the good shepherd, and know my sheep, and am known of mine. As the Father knoweth me, even so know I the Father: and I lay down my life for the sheep. And other sheep I have which are not of this fold; them also must I bring, and they shall hear my voice and there shall be one fold and one shepherd.

And that done, the President shall say unto them as hereafter followeth:

You have heard, brethren, as well in your private examination as in the exhortation which was now made to you, and in the holy lessons taken out of the Gospel, and the writings of the Apostles, of what dignity and of how great importance this office is whereunto you are called. And now again we exhort you, in the name of our Lord Jesus Christ, that you have in remembrance into how high a dignity, and to how weighty an office ye are called. That is to say, to be messengers, watchmen, and stewards of the Lord, to teach and to premonish, to feed and provide for the Lord's family, to seek for Christ's sheep that are dispersed abroad, and for his children who are in the midst of this evil world, that they may be saved through Christ for ever.

Have always, therefore, in remembrance how great a treasure is committed to your charge. For they are the sheep of Christ, which he bought with his death, and for whom he shed his blood. The church and congregation whom you must serve, is his spouse, and his body. And if it shall happen the same church, or any member thereof, do take any hurt or hindrance by reason of your negligence, ye know the greatness of the fault, and also the horrible punishment that will ensue. Wherefore consider with yourselves the end of the Ministry towards the children of God, towards the spouse and body of Christ; and see that you never cease your labour, your care and diligence, until you have done all that lieth in you, according to your bounden duty, to bring all such as are or shall be committed to your charge, unto that agreement in the faith and knowledge of God, and to that ripeness and perfectness of age in Christ, that there be no place left among you either for error in religion or for viciousness in life.

Forasmuch, then, as your office is both of so great excellency and of so great difficulty, ye see with how great care and study ye ought to apply yourselves, as well that ye may show yourselves dutiful and thankful unto that Lord who hath placed you in so high a dignity, as also to beware that neither you yourselves offend, nor be occasion that others offend. Howbeit ye cannot have a mind and will thereto of yourselves; for that will and ability is given of God alone: Therefore ye ought, and have need to pray earnestly for his Holy Spirit. And seeing that ye cannot compass the doing of so weighty a work, pertaining to the salvation of man, but with doctrine and exhortation taken out of the Holy Scriptures, and with a life agreeable to the same; consider how studious ye ought to be in reading and learning the Scriptures, and in framing the manners both of yourselves and of them that specially pertain unto you, according to the rule of the same Scriptures; and, for this self-same cause, how ye ought to forsake and set aside (as much as you may) all worldly cares and studies.

We have good hope that you have all weighed and pondered these things long before this time; and that you have clearly determined, by God's grace, to give yourselves wholly to this office whereunto it hath pleased God to call you; so that, as much as lieth in you, you will apply yourselves wholly to this one thing, and draw all your cares and studies this way, and that you will continue to pray to God the Father, by the mediation of our only Saviour, Jesus Christ, for the heavenly assistance of the Holy Ghost, that, by the daily reading and weighing of the Scriptures, ye may wax riper and stronger in your Ministry; and that ye may so endeavor yourselves, from time to time, to sanctify the lives of you and yours, and to fashion them after the rule and doctrine of Christ, that ye may be wholesome and godly examples and patterns for the people to follow.

And now that this present congregation of Christ here

assembled may also understand your minds and wills in these things, and that this your promise may the more move you to do your duties,—ye shall answer plainly to these things which we, in the name of God and his Church, shall demand of you touching the same.

Do you think, in heart, that you are truly called, according to the will of our Lord Jesus Christ, to the office of a Minister?

Ans. I think so.

The President. Are you persuaded that the Holy Scriptures contain sufficiently all doctrine required of necessity for eternal salvation through faith in Jesus Christ? and are you determined out of the said Scriptures to instruct the people committed to your charge, and to teach nothing as required of necessity to eternal salvation but that which you shall be persuaded may be concluded and proved by the Scriptures?

Ans. I am so persuaded, and have so determined, by God's grace.

The President. Will you then give your faithful diligence always so to minister the Doctrines, and Sacraments, and Discipline of Christ, as the Lord hath commanded?

Ans. I will so do, by the help of the Lord.

The President. Will you be ready, with all faithful diligence, to banish and drive away all erroneous and strange doctrines contrary to God's word; and to use both public and private monitions and exhortations, as well to the sick as to the whole within your charge, as need shall require and occasion shall be given?

Ans. I will, the Lord being my helper.

The President. Will you be diligent in prayers and in reading of the Holy Scriptures, and in such studies as help to the knowledge of the same, laying aside the study of the world and the flesh.

Ans. I will endeavor so to do, the Lord being my helper.

The President. Will you be diligent to frame and fashion yourselves, and your families, according to the doctrines of Christ; and to make both yourselves and them, as much as in you lieth, wholesome examples and patterns to the flock of Christ?

Ans. I shall apply myself thereto, the Lord being my helper.

The President. Will you maintain and set forward, as much as lieth in you, quietness, peace, and love among all Christian people, and especially among them that are or shall be committed to your charge?

Ans. I will so do, the Lord being my helper.

The President. Will you reverently obey your chief Ministers, unto whom is committed the charge and government over you; following with a glad mind and will their godly admonitions, submitting yourself to their godly judgments?

Ans. I will so do, the Lord being my helper.

Then shall the President, standing up, say:

Almighty God, who hath given you this will to do all these things, grant also unto you strength and power to perform the same; that he may accomplish his work which he hath begun in you, through Jesus Christ our Lord. *Amen.*

[After this the congregation shall be desired, secretly in their prayers, to make their humble supplications to God for all these things, for the which prayers there shall be silence kept for a space.]

After which shall be said by the President, (the persons to be ordained Ministers all kneeling,) Veni, Creator, Spiritus, the President beginning, and the Ministers and others that are present answering by verse, as followeth:

> Come, Holy Ghost, our souls inspire,
> *And lighten with celestial fire.*
> Thou the anointing Spirit art,
> *Who dost thy Seven-fold gifts impart.*
> Thy blessed Unction from above,
> *Is comfort, life, and fire of love.*
> Enable with perpetual light,
> *The dullness of our blinded sight.*
> Anoint and cheer our soilèd face
> *With the abundance of thy grace;*
> Keep far our foes, give peace at home,
> *Where thou art guide, no ill can come.*
> Teach us to know the Father, Son,
> *And Thee, of both to be but one:*
> That through the ages all along,
> *This may be our endless song;*
> Praise to thy eternal merit,
> *Father, Son, and Holy Spirit.*

That done, the President shall pray in this wise:

Almighty God and heavenly Father, who of thine infinite love and goodness towards us, hast given to us thy only and most dearly beloved Son Jesus Christ to be our Redeemer and the Author of everlasting life; who, after he had made perfect our redemption by his death, and was ascended into heaven, sent abroad into the world his Apostles, Prophets, Evangelists, Pastors, and Teachers; by whose labour and ministry he gathered together a great flock in all parts of the world, to set forth the eternal praise of thy holy name; for these, so great benefits of thy eternal goodness, and for that thou hast vouchsafed to call these thy servants here present to the same office and ministry appointed for the salvation of mankind, we render unto thee most hearty thanks: We praise and worship thee; and we humbly beseech thee, by the same thy blessed Son, to grant unto all, who either here or elsewhere call upon thy name, that we may continue to show ourselves thankful unto thee for these and all other thy benefits, and that we may daily increase and go forward in the knowledge and faith of thee and thy Son, by the Holy Spirit. So that, as well by these thy Ministers, as by them over whom they shall be appointed thy Ministers, thy holy name may be for ever glorified, and thy blessed kingdom enlarged, through the same thy Son Jesus Christ our Lord; who liveth and reigneth with thee in the unity of the same Holy Spirit, world without end. *Amen.*

When this prayer is ended, the President, with two or more of the Ministers present, shall lay their hands severally upon the head of every one that receiveth the order of Ministers; the Receivers humbly kneeling upon their knees, and the President saying:

The Lord pour upon thee the Holy Ghost for the office and work of a Minister in the Church of God, now committed unto thee by the imposition of our hands. And be thou a faithful Dispenser of the Word of God, and of his Holy Sacraments; in the name of the Father, and of the Son, and of the Holy Ghost. *Amen.*

Then the President shall deliver to every one of them, kneeling, the Bible into his hands, saying:

Take thou authority to preach the Word of God, and to administer the Holy Sacraments in the congregation.

Then the President shall say:

Most merciful Father, we beseech thee to send upon these thy servants thy heavenly blessing, that they may be clothed with righteousness, and that thy Word spoken by their mouths may have such success that it may never be spoken in vain. Grant also that we may have grace to hear and receive what they shall deliver out of thy most Holy Word, or agreeably to the same, as the means of our salvation; and that, in all our words and deeds, we may seek thy glory and the increase of thy kingdom, through Jesus Christ our Lord. *Amen.*

Prevent us, O Lord, in all our doings, with thy most gracious favour, and further us with thy continual help, that, in all our works begun, continued, and ended in thee, we may glorify thy holy name, and finally, by thy mercy, obtain everlasting life, through Jesus Christ our Lord. *Amen.*

The peace of God that passeth all understanding, keep your hearts and minds in the knowledge and love of God, and of his Son Jesus Christ our Lord; and the blessings of God Almighty, the Father, the Son, and the Holy Ghost, be among you, and remain with you always. *Amen.*

Section V.

THE FORM OF SOLEMNIZATION OF MATRIMONY.

First, the Banns of all that are to be married together must be published in the Congregation three several Sundays, in the time of Divine Service, (unless they be otherwise qualified according to law,) the Minister saying, after the accustomed manner:

I publish the Banns of Marriage between M of ———, and N of ———. If any of you know cause or just impediment why these two persons should not be joined together in holy Matrimony, *ye* are to declare it. This is the first [*second* or *third*] time of asking.

At the time appointed for the solemnization of Matrimony, the Persons to be married standing together, the man at the right hand of the woman, the Minister shall say:

Dearly beloved, we are gathered together here, in the sight of God, and in the presence of these witnesses, to join together this Man and this Woman in holy Matrimony, which is an honourable estate, instituted of God in the time of man's innocency, signifying unto us the mystical union that is betwixt Christ and his Church; which holy estate Christ adorned and beautified with his presence, and the first miracle that he wrought in Cana of Galilee, and is commended of St. Paul to be honorable among all men; and therefore is not by any to be enterprised or taken in hand unadvisedly, but reverently, discreetly, advisedly, and in the fear of God.

Into which holy estate these two persons present come now to be joined. Therefore, if any one can show any just cause why they may not lawfully be joined together, let him now speak, or else hereafter for ever hold his peace.

And also speaking unto the Persons that are to be married, he shall say:

I require and charge you both, (as you will answer at the dreadful day of judgment, when the secrets of all hearts shall be disclosed), that if either of you know any impediment why you may not be lawfully joined together in Matrimony, you do now confess it. For be ye well assured, that so many as are coupled together otherwise than as God's word doth allow, are not joined together by God, neither is their Matrimony lawful.

If no impediment be alleged, then shall the Minister say unto the Man:

M, Wilt thou have this Woman to be thy wedded Wife, to live together after God's ordinance, in the holy estate of Matrimony? Wilt thou love her, comfort her, honour and keep her, in sickness and in health; and, forsaking all other, keep thee only unto her, so long as ye both shall live?

The Man shall answer:

I will.

Then shall the Minister say unto the Woman:

N, Wilt thou have this Man to be thy wedded Husband, to live together after God's ordinance, in the holy estate of Matrimony? Wilt thou obey him, serve him, love, honour, and keep him, in sickness and in health; and, forsaking all other, keep thee only unto him, so long as ye both shall live?

The Woman shall answer:

I will.

Then the Minister shall cause the Man with his right hand to take the Woman by her right hand, and to say after him, as followeth:

I *M*, take thee *N*, to be my wedded Wife, to have and to hold, from this day forward, for better for worse, for richer for poorer, in sickness and in health, to love and to cherish, till death us do part, according to God's holy ordinance; and thereto I plight thee my faith.

Then shall they loose their hands, and the Woman, with her right hand, taking the Man by his right hand, shall likewise say after the Minister:

I *N*, take thee *M*, to be my wedded Husband, to have and to hold, from this day forward, for better for worse, for richer for poorer, in sickness and in health, to love, cherish, and to obey, till death us do part, according to God's holy ordinance; and thereto I give thee my faith.

When the parties desire to be married with a ring, the following form may be used;—The Man placing the ring upon the fourth finger of the Woman's left hand, shall say after the Minister:

With this Ring, a token and pledge of the Vow and Covenant now made between me and thee, I do thee wed, in the Name of the Father, and of the Son, and of the Holy Ghost.

Then shall the Minister say—Let us Pray:

O Eternal God, Creator and Preserver of all Mankind, Giver of all Spiritual Grace, the Author of Everlasting Life; send thy blessing upon these thy servants, this Man and this Woman, whom we bless in thy name; that as Isaac and Rebecca lived faithfully together, so these persons may surely perform and keep the vow and covenant betwixt them made, and may ever remain in perfect love and peace together, and live according to thy laws, through Jesus Christ our Lord. *Amen.*

Then shall the Minister join their right hands together and say:

Those whom God hath joined together let no man put asunder.

Forasmuch as *M* and *N* have consented together in holy wedlock, and have witnessed the same before God and this company, and thereto have pledged their faith either to other, and have declared the same by joining of hands, and by the giving and receiving of a ring, I pronounce that they are Husband and Wife together,—In the name of the Father, and of the Son, and of the Holy Ghost. *Amen.*

And the Minister shall add this blessing:

God the Father, God the Son, God the Holy Ghost, bless, preserve, and keep you; the Lord mercifully with his favour look upon you, and so fill you with all spiritual benediction and grace, that ye may so live together in this life that in the world to come ye may have life everlasting. *Amen.*

Then the Minister shall say:

Our Father who art in heaven, Hallowed be thy name, Thy kingdom come. Thy will be done on earth as it is in heaven. Give us this day our daily bread. And forgive us our trespasses, as we forgive them that trespass against us. And lead us not into temptation, but deliver us from evil. *Amen.*

Then shall the Minister say:

O God of Abraham, God of Isaac, God of Jacob, bless this Man and this Woman, and sow the seed of eternal life in their hearts, that whatsoever in thy holy word they shall profitably learn, they may indeed fulfil the same. Look, O Lord, mercifully on them from heaven, and bless them. And as thou didst send thy blessings upon Abraham and Sarah, to their great comfort; so vouchsafe to send thy blessings upon this Man and this Woman, that they, obeying thy will, and always being in safety under thy protection, may abide in thy love unto their lives' end, through Jesus Christ our Lord. *Amen.*

O God, who by thy mighty power hast made all things of

nothing, who also (after other things set in order) didst appoint that out of man (created after thine own image and similitude) woman should take her beginning, and, knitting them together, didst teach that it should never be lawful to put asunder those whom thou by Matrimony hast made one; O God, who hast consecrated the state of Matrimony to such an excellent mystery that in it is signified and represented the spiritual marriage and unity betwixt Christ and his Church, look mercifully upon this Man and this Woman; that this Man may love his Wife according to thy Word, (as Christ did love his Spouse, the Church, who gave himself for it, loving and cherishing it, even as his own flesh;) and also that this Woman may be loving and amiable, faithful and obedient to her husband; and in all quietness, sobriety and peace, be a follower of holy and godly matrons. O Lord, bless them both, and grant them to inherit thy everlasting kingdom, through Jesus Christ our Lord. *Amen.*

Then shall the Minister say:

Almighty God, who at the beginning did create our first parents, Adam and Eve, and did sanctify and join them together in marriage, pour upon you the riches of his grace, sanctify and bless you, that ye may please him both in body and soul, and live together in holy love, unto your lives' end. *Amen.*

Section VI.

THE ORDER OF THE BURIAL OF THE DEAD.

[N.B. The following or some other solemn service shall be used:]
The Minister meeting the Corpse, and going before it, shall say:

I am the resurrection and the life, saith the Lord; he that believeth in me, though he were dead, yet shall he live;

and whosoever liveth and believeth in me, shall never die. John xi. 25, 26.

I know that my Redeemer liveth, and that he shall stand at the latter day upon the earth: And though after my skin worms destroy this body, yet in my flesh shall I see God: whom I shall see for myself, and mine eyes shall behold, and not another. Job xix. 25, 26, 27.

We brought nothing into this world, and it is certain we can carry nothing out. The Lord gave, and the Lord hath taken away; blessed be the name of the Lord. 1 Tim. vi. 7; Job i. 21.

At the grave, when the Corpse is laid in the earth, the Minister shall say:

Man that is born of a woman hath but a short time to live, and is full of misery. He cometh up and is cut down like a flower; he fleeth as it were a shadow, and never continueth in one stay.

In the midst of life we are in death; of whom may we seek for succour, but of thee, O Lord, who for our sins art justly displeased.

Yet, O Lord God most holy, O Lord most mighty, O holy and most merciful Saviour, deliver us not into the bitter pains of eternal death.

Thou knowest, Lord, the secrets of our hearts; shut not thy merciful ears to our prayers, but spare us, Lord most holy, O God most mighty, O holy and merciful Saviour, thou most worthy Judge eternal, suffer us not at our last hour, for any pains of death, to fall from thee.

Then, while the earth shall be cast upon the body by some standing by, the Minister shall say,

Forasmuch as it hath pleased Almighty God in his infinite wisdom to remove the departed from among us, we now commit [*his*] body to the ground, earth to earth, ashes to ashes, dust to dust, awaiting the resurrection of the dead at the last great day.

Then shall be said:

I heard a voice from heaven saying unto me, Write, Blessed are the dead which die in the Lord from henceforth : Yea, saith the Spirit, that they may rest from their labours ; and their works do follow them.

Then shall the Minister say :

Lord have mercy upon us,
Christ have mercy upon us,
Lord have mercy upon us,

Our Father which art in heaven, hallowed be thy name. Thy kingdom come. Thy will be done on earth as it is in heaven. Give us this day our daily bread. And forgive us our trespasses, as we forgive them that trespass against us. And lead us not into temptation ; but deliver us from evil. *Amen.*

The Collect.

O merciful God, the Father of our Lord Jesus Christ, who is the resurrection and the life; in whom whosoever believeth shall live, though he die ; and whosoever liveth and believeth in him shall not die eternally :—We meekly beseech thee, O Father, to raise us from the death of sin unto the life of righteousness ; that when we shall depart this life we may rest in him ; and, at the general resurrection on the last day, may be found acceptable in thy sight, and receive that blessing which thy well-beloved Son shall then pronounce to all that love and fear thee, saying, Come ye blessed children of my Father, receive the kingdom prepared for you from the beginning of the world. Grant this, we beseech thee, O merciful Father, through Jesus Christ our Mediator and Redeemer. *Amen.*

The Grace of our Lord Jesus Christ, and the love of God, and the fellowship of the Holy Ghost, be with us all evermore. *Amen.*

Section VII.

THE FORM OF RENEWING THE COVENANT.

[After a short sermon, impressing upon every soul the importance of giving himself to God, and that without delay, each Preacher is recommended, on his first tour round his Circuit in the New Year, beginning the first Sabbath in January, to read the following directions, or some of them, in every congregation, and persuade as many as possible to make solemn Covenant with God, and by Divine grace, to keep the Covenant inviolate unto the day of His coming :]

I. Get these three principles fixed in your heart : That things eternal are much more considerable than things temporal ; that things not seen are as certain as the things that are seen ; that upon your present choice depends your eternal lot. Choose Christ and his ways, and you are blessed for ever ; refuse, and you are undone for ever. And then,

II. Make your choice.

Turn either to the right hand or to the left ; lay both parts before you, with every link of each ; Christ with his yoke, his cross, and his crown ; or, the devil, with his wealth, his pleasure, and curse ; and then put yourselves to it thus : " Soul, thou seest what is before thee : what wilt thou do ? Which wilt thou have, either the crown or the curse ? If thou choosest the crown, remember that the day thou takest this, thou must be content to submit to the cross and yoke, the service and the sufferings of Christ, which are linked to it. What sayest thou ? Hadst thou rather take the gains and pleasures of sin, and venture on the curse? Or wilt thou yield thyself to Christ, and so make sure of the crown?"

If your hearts fly off, and would fain waive the business, leave them not so. If you be unresolved, you are resolved; if you remain undetermined for Christ, you are determined for the devil. Therefore, give not off, but follow your hearts from day to day; let them not rest till the matter be brought to an issue; and see that you make a good choice.

This is your choosing the good part, God and the blessedness of the world to come, for your portion and happiness; and in this is included your renouncing the world and worldly happiness.

III. Embark with Christ.

Adventure yourselves with him; cast yourselves upon his righteousness, as that which shall bring you to God; as a poor captive exile that is cast upon a strange land, a land of robbers and murderers, where he is ready to perish, and having no hope, either of abiding there, or of escaping home with life; and meeting at length with a pilot, that offers to transport him safely home, he embarks with him, and ventures himself, and all he hath, in his vessel. Do you likewise: you are exiles from the presence of God, and fallen into the hands of robbers and murderers; your sins are robbers, your pleasures are robbers, your companions are robbers and thieves. If you stay where you are you perish; and escape home of yourself you cannot. Christ offers, if you will venture with him, he will bring you home, he will bring you to God. Will you now say to him, "Lord Jesus, wilt thou undertake for me? Wilt thou bring me to God, bring me into the Land of Promise?

With thee will I venture myself; I cast myself upon thee, upon thy blood, and thy righteousness; I lay up all my hopes, and venture my whole interest, soul and body, with thee.

This is closing with Christ as your Priest. And in this is included your renouncing your own righteousness: you can never, you will never, cast yourselves on him alone, till all your hopes in yourselves have given up the ghost.

There are two things which must necessarily be supposed, in order to a sinner's coming to Christ:

1. A deep sense of his sin and misery.
2. An utter despair of himself, and all things else besides Christ.

1. A deep sense of sin and misery.

No man will regard a Saviour that doth not see himself a sinner; the whole regard not the physician. Therefore, it is said, that the Spirit of God, when he should come to christianize the world, should, in the first place, "convince the world of sin." (John xvi. 8.) He shall convince the world of sin; he shall demonstrate them sinners, bring up their sins before their eyes; bring home their sins upon their consciences, and make them see them, and feel themselves most vile and filthy. Sin hides itself from the sinner's eyes, and all its vileness and deformity. But the Spirit of God plucks off the mantle, and makes sin appear to be sin; makes all the sinner's gods appear to be as so many devils; brings forth the blackness and filthiness of sin into sight, and makes the sinner see himself an unclean and abominable creature; and, withal, he brings forth the guilt of sin, awakens the sinner's conscience, and fills him with fear, terror, and amazement. In this respect he is called the Spirit of bondage, that works fear and trouble in the heart. The Spirit's awakening a sleepy sinner, is a kind of awakening in hell. "Lord what am I? What mean these legions round about me, these chains and fetters that are upon me? What means this black roll before mine eyes, of curses, and wrath, and woes? Lord, where am I? Have I been playing and sporting, and making merry, and my soul in such a case as this? But is there no hope of escaping out of this wretched state? I see there is no abiding thus. I am but a dead man, if I continue as I am. What must I do to be saved?"

When he is brought to this, there is some way made for his entertainment with Christ; yet this is not all that is needful, but he further must be brought to,

2. An utter despair of himself, and all things else without Christ.

Being made sensible of his sin and his danger, a sinner will look for help and deliverance; but he will look every where else before he will look unto Christ; nothing will bring a sinner to Christ but absolute necessity. He will try to forsake his sins, and to see if by these means he may escape. He will have recourse to prayers, and sermons, and sacraments, and search if there be not salvation in them. But all these, though they be useful in their places, and indeed necessary, yet, looking no further, the sinner sees there is no salvation in them; his righteousness cannot save him,—this is but rags; his duties cannot save him,—these may be reckoned among his sins; ordinances cannot save him,—these are but empty cisterns; and all tell him, "You knock at a wrong door; salvation is not in us." "Well, the Lord be merciful unto me," saith the sinner, "What shall I do? Abide as I am I dare not, and how to help myself I know not: my praying will not save me; my hearing will not; if I give all my goods to the poor, if I should give my body to be burned, all this would not save my soul. Woe is me! what shall I do, and whither shall I go?"

And now being brought to this distress, to this utter loss, his despair drives him to the only door of hope that is left open. Then Christ will be acceptable, when he sees none but Christ can save him. The Apostle tells us, "We are kept under the law, shut up unto the faith that should afterwards be revealed." (Gal. iii. 23.) All other doors were shut up against us; there was no hope of escaping but by that one door which was left open. "The faith that was afterwards to be revealed."- As the besieged in a city, that have every gate blocked up, and but one difficult passage left open, by which there is any possibility of escaping, thither throng for the saving of their lives; they are shut up unto that door, to which (if there had been any other way open) they would never have come.

And as Christ will never be accepted, so can the sinner never be received of him, till he lets go all other props, and trusts in Him alone. Christ will have no sharer with him in the work of saving souls. "If ye seek me, let these go their way," as he said in another case; let not only your sins go, but all dependance on your righteousness, all the refuge of lies wherein you have trusted; let all go, if you will have me to be a refuge to you. I came not to call the righteous; if I should, they would not come; or if they come, let them go as they came, let them go to their righteousness in which they trust; and let naked, destitute sinners, distressed sinners, come to me; who am come to this end, to seek and to save them that are lost.

Sinners, will you come now? Will you venture here?

For this your adventuring on Christ, you have this threefold warrant:—

1. God's Ordination. This is he whom God the Father hath appointed, and sent into the world, to bring back his exiles to himself, to save sinners. This is he whom God the Father hath sealed, hath marked him out for that chosen person in whom is salvation; hath sealed him his commission, for the redeeming and reconciling the world to himself. As God said unto the three friends of Job, when he was angry with them, "Go to my servant Job, and he shall offer sacrifice for you; he shall pray for you, for him will I accept." (Job xlii. 8.) So to sinners: Go, saith the Lord, to my servant Jesus; he shall offer sacrifice for you, he shall make reconciliation for you. "Behold my servant whom I uphold, mine Elect in whom my soul delighteth; I have put my Spirit upon him, he shall bring forth judgment to the Gentiles." (Isaiah xlii. 1.)

2. God's command, "This is his commandment, That we should believe on the name of his Son Jesus Christ." (1 John iii. 23.

3. The promise of God: "Behold, I lay in Sion a chief corner-stone, elect, precious: he that believeth on him shall not be confounded." (1 Pet. ii. 6.)

Now, having this three-fold warrant—the warrant of God's ordination, command, and promise—you may be bold to adventure on Christ, and to apply yourself to him thus: "Lord Jesus, here I am, a poor captive exile, a lost creature, an enemy to God, under his wrath and curse. Wilt thou, Lord, undertake for me, reconcile me to God, and save my soul? Do not, Lord, refuse me; for if thou refuse me, to whom then shall I go? Art not thou he, and he alone, whom God the Father hath sealed, the Saviour of sinners? The

Lord God hath sent me to thee, hath bid me come; he hath commanded me to believe, and cast myself upon thee. Lord Jesus, wilt thou refuse to help a distressed creature, whom the Father hath sent to thee for thy help? If I had come on my own head, or in my own name, thou mightest well have put me back; but since I come at the command of the Father, reject me not! Lord, help me! Lord, save me! Art thou not he, concerning whom the Father hath promised, 'He that believeth on him shall not be confounded?' I come, Lord; I believe, Lord; I throw myself upon thy grace and mercy; I cast myself upon thy blood. Do not refuse me. I have no where else to go. Here I will stay, I will not stir from thy door; on thee will I trust, and rest and venture myself. God hath laid my help on thee, and on thee I lay my hope for pardon, for life, for salvation. If I perish, I perish on thy shoulders; if I sink, I sink on thy vessel; if I die, I die at thy door.

IV. Resign and deliver up yourselves to God in Christ.

"Yield yourselves to the Lord," that is, as his servants; give up the dominion and government of yourselves to Christ. "Neither yield your members as instruments of unrighteousness unto sin; but yield yourselves to God, as those that are alive from the dead, and your members as instruments of righteousness unto God. "To whom ye yield yourselves servants to obey, his servants ye are to whom ye obey." Yield yourselves so to the Lord, that you may henceforth be the Lord's: "I am thine," says the Psalmist. Those that yield themselves to sin and the world, their heart says, "Sin, I am thine: world, I am thine;—riches, I am yours; pleasures, I am yours." "I am thine," saith the Psalmist; devoted to thy fear, dedicated to thy service. "I am thine, save me." Give yourselves to Christ, sinners; be devoted to his fear.

And this giving yourselves to him must be such as supposes that ye be heartily contented,—

1. That he appoint you your work.
2. That he appoint you your station.

1. That he appoint you your work: That he put you to whatsoever he pleaseth. Servants, as they must do their master's work, so they must do that work which their master appoints them; they must be for any work their master hath for them to do; they must not pick and choose; "This I will do, and that I will not do:" they must not say, "This is too hard," or "This is too mean, or "This may be well enough let alone." Good servants, when they have chosen their master, will let their master choose their work; and will not dispute his will, but do it.

Christ hath many services to be done; some are more easy and honorable, others more difficult and disagreeable; some are suitable to our inclinations and interests, others are contrary to both. In some we may please Christ, and please ourselves; as, when he requires us to feed and clothe ourselves, to provide things honest for our maintenance. Yea, and there are some spiritual duties that are more pleasing than others; as, to rejoice in the Lord, to be blessing and praising God, to be feeding ourselves with the delights and comforts of religion: these are the sweet works of a Christian. But then there are other works, wherein we cannot please Christ but by denying ourselves; as, giving and lending, bearing and forbearing, reproving men for their sins, withdrawing from their company, witnessing against their wickedness, confessing Christ and his name, when it will cause us shame and reproach; sailing against the wind, swimming against the tide, steering contrary to the times, parting with our ease, our liberties, and our accommodations for the name of our Lord Jesus.

> It is desirable that the whole of this Tract be prayerfully pondered in private by those who purpose to enter into the Covenant; but, to shorten the service, the Preachers may here begin to read, on occasion of the annual renewal of the Covenant in the Methodist Societies.]

It is necessary, beloved, to sit down, and consider what it will cost you to be the servants of Christ, and take a thorough survey of the whole business of Christianity, and not to engage thoughtlessly to you know not what.

First, see what it is that Christ doth expect, and then yield yourselves to his whole will. Do not think of compounding or making your own terms with Christ: that will never be allowed you.

Go to Christ, and tell him, "Lord Jesus, if thou wilt receive me into thy house, if thou wilt but own me as thy servant, I will not stand upon terms; impose upon me what conditions thou pleasest, write down thine own articles, command me what thou wilt, put me to any thing thou seest good; let me come under thy roof, let me be thy servant, and spare not to command me: I will be no longer mine own, but give up myself to thy will in all things."

2. Let him appoint you your station and condition; whether it be higher or lower, a prosperous or afflicted state. Be content that Christ should choose your work and choose your condition; that he should have the command of you, and the disposal of you: "Make me what thou wilt, Lord, and set me where thou wilt: let me be a vessel of silver or gold, or a vessel of wood or stone, so I be a vessel of honour: of whatsoever form or metal, whether higher or lower, finer

or coarser, I am content; if I be not the head, or the eye, or the ear, one of the nobler and more honourable instruments thou wilt employ, let me be the hand, or the foot, one of the most laborious, the lowest, and most contemptible of all the servants of my Lord; let my dwelling be in the dust, my portion in the wilderness, my name and lot amongst the hewers of wood and drawers of water, among the door-keepers of thy house; anywhere, where I may be serviceable. I put myself wholly into thy hands; put me to what thou wilt, rank me with whom thou wilt; put me to doing; put me to suffering; let me be employed for thee, or laid aside for thee; exalted for thee, or trodden under foot for thee; let me be full, let me be empty; let me have all things, let me have nothing; I freely and heartily resign all to thy pleasure and disposal."

This is closing with Christ as your King and Sovereign Lord; and in this is included your renouncing the devil and all his works, the flesh and its lusts; together with your consenting to all the laws and ordinances of Christ and his providential Government.

Beloved, such an agreement with Christ as you have here been exhorted to, is that wherein the essence of Christianity lies. When you have chosen the incorruptible crown; that is, when you have chosen God to be your portion and happiness; when you have adventured, and laid up your whole interest and all your hopes with Christ, casting yourself wholly upon the merits of his death; when you have understandingly and heartily resigned yourselves to him, resolving for ever to be at his command, and at his disposal; then you are Christians indeed, and never till then. Christ will be the Saviour of none but his servants. He is the Author of eternal salvation to those that obey him; Christ will have no servants but by consent; his people are a willing people; Christ will accept of no consent but *in full* to all he requires; he will be all in all, or he will be nothing.

V. Confirm and complete all this by solemn covenant.

Give yourselves to the Lord as his servants, and bind yourselves to him as his covenant servants.

Upon your entering into covenant with God, the covenant of God stands firm to you : God gives you leave, every one, to put in his own name into the covenant-grant; if it be not found there at last, it will be your own fault; if it be not there, there will be nothing found in the whole covenant belonging unto you; if it be there, all is your's; if you have come into the bond of the covenant, you shall have your share in the blessings of the covenant. "Thou hast avouched the Lord this day to be thy God, to walk in his ways, and to keep his statutes, and his commandments, and his judgments, to hearken to his voice; and the Lord hath avouched thee this day to be his peculiar people, as he hath promised thee." (Deut. xxvi. 17, 18.) Observe it: The same day that they avouched the Lord to be their God, the same day the Lord avouched them to be his peculiar people. The same day that they engaged to keep the commandments of God, the same day the Lord engageth to keep his promise with them.

There is a two-fold covenanting with God. In *profession*, or in *reality;* an entering our names, or an engaging our hearts. The former is done in baptism, by all that are baptized, who, by receiving that seal of the Covenant, are visibly, or in profession, entered into it. The latter is also two-fold.

1. VIRTUAL. Which is done by all those that have sincerely made that closure with God in Christ, which we have spoken of. Those that have chosen the Lord, embarked

with Christ, resigned up, and given themselves to the Lord, have virtually covenanted with him.

2. FORMAL. Which is our binding ourselves to the Lord by solemn vow or promise to stand to our choice. And this may be either inward in the soul, or outward, and expressed either by word, lifting up the hands, subscribing with the hand, or the like; and by how much the more express and solemn our covenanting with God is, by so much the more sensibly and strongly is it likely to hold our hearts to him.

Now, that which we would persuade you to, is this solemn and express covenanting with God; and in order to the putting this matter into practice, take these few directions:—

1. Seek earnestly his special assistance, and gracious acceptance of you.

2. Consider distinctly all the conditions of the Covenant, as they have been laid before you.

3. Search your hearts, whether you either have already or can now freely make such a closure with God in Christ, as you have been exhorted to. Especially consider what your sins are, and examine whether you can resolve to forego them all. Consider what the laws of Christ are, how holy, strict, and spiritual, and whether you can, upon deliberation, make choice of them all, (even those that most cross your interests and corrupt inclinations), as the rule of your whole life. Be sure you be clear in these matters; see that you do not lie unto God.

Secondly, Compose your spirits into the most serious frame possible, suitable to a transaction of so high importance.

Thirdly, Lay hold on the covenant of God, and rely upon His promise of giving grace and strength, whereby you may be enabled to perform your promise. Trust not to your own strength, or to the strength of your own resolutions, but take hold on His strength.

Fourthly, Resolve to be faithful. Having engaged your hearts, opened your mouths, and subscribed with your hands to the Lord, resolve in His strength never to go back.

[Here let the Minister request all who are willing to engage in the renewal of the Covenant, to signify it by standing up, after which, in the name of the congregation, he shall open his lips to the Lord, in these words, all devoutly kneeling.]

O most holy and most merciful God! for the passion of thy Son, we beseech thee accept of us poor prodigals now prostrating ourselves at thy door. We have fallen from thee by our iniquity and are by nature heirs of death, and a thousand-fold more children of hell by our sinful practice; but of Thine infinite grace Thou hast promised mercy to us in Christ, if we will but turn to thee with all our hearts; therefore, upon the call of thy Gospel, we are now come in, and, throwing down our weapons, submit ourselves to thy mercy.

And because thou requirest, as the condition of our peace with thee, that we should put away our idols, and be at defiance with all thine enemies, which, we acknowledge, we have wickedly sided with against thee, we here, from the bottom of our hearts, renounce them all; firmly covenanting with thee not to allow ourselves in any known sin, but conscientiously to use all the means that we know thou hast prescribed for the death and utter destruction of all our corruptions. And whereas, formerly, we have inordinately let out our affections upon the world, we do here resign our hearts to thee; humbly protesting before thy glorious Majesty, that it is our firm resolution, and that we do unfeignedly desire grace from thee, that when thou shalt call us hereunto, we may practice this our resolution, to forsake all that is dear unto us in this world, rather than turn from thee to the ways of sin; and that we will watch against all temptations, whether of prosperity or adversity, lest they should withdraw our hearts from thee, beseeching thee also to help us against the temptations of Satan, to whose wicked suggestions we resolve, by thy grace, never to yield. And because our own righteousness is but filthy rags, we renounce all confidence therein; and acknowledge that we are of ourselves hopeless, helpless, undone creatures, without righteousness or strength.

And forasmuch as thou hast, of thy boundless mercy, offered most graciously to us, wretched sinners, to be again our God through Christ, if we would accept of thee; we call heaven and earth to record this day, that we do here solemnly avouch thee for the Lord our God; and with all possible veneration, bowing our souls under the feet of thy most sacred Majesty, we do here give up ourselves to thee, the Lord Jehovah, Father, Son, and Holy Ghost, for thy servants; promising and vowing to serve thee, in holiness and righteousness, all the days of our lives.

And since thou hast appointed the Lord Jesus Christ the only means of coming unto thee, we do here, upon our bended knees, accept of Him, as the only new and living way by which sinners may have access to thee.

O blessed Jesus, we come to thee hungry, wretched, miserable, blind, and naked; guilty, condemned malefactors, unworthy to wash the feet of the servants of our Lord, much more to be joined in covenant to the King of Glory; but since such is thine unparalleled love, we here, with all our power, accept thee, and take thee for our head and Lord; for better, for worse; for richer, for poorer; for all times and conditions, to love, honour, and obey thee before all others, and this to the death. We embrace thee in all thy offices; we renounce our own worthiness, and do here avow thee for the Lord, our righteousness; we renounce our own wisdom, and do here take thee for our only guide; we renounce our own will, and do take thy will for our law.

And since thou hast told us we must suffer if we will reign, we do here covenant with thee, to take our lot as it falls with thee, and, by thy grace assisting, to run all hazards with thee; verily purposing, that neither life nor death shall part between thee and us.

And because thou hast been pleased to give us thy holy laws as the rule of our lives, and the way in which we should walk to thy kingdom, we do here willingly put ourselves under thy yoke, and set our shoulders to thy burden; and, subscribing to all thy laws, as holy, just, and good, we solemnly take them as the rule of our words, thoughts, and actions; promising that, though our flesh contradict and rebel, we will endeavour to order and govern our whole lives according to thy direction.

[Here shall follow a season of silent prayer. Then the whole congregation, led by the Minister, shall repeat audibly the following words:]

Now, Almighty God, Searcher of Hearts, thou knowest that I make this covenant with thee this day without any known guile or reservation, beseeching thee, if thou espiest any flaw or falsehood therein, that thou wouldst discover it to me, and help me to do it aright.

And now, glory be to thee, O God the Father, whom I shall be bold, from this day forward, to look upon as my

God and Father, that ever thou shouldst find out such a way for the recovery of undone sinners. Glory be to thee, O God the Son, who hast loved me, and washed me from my sins in thine own blood, and art now become my Saviour and Redeemer.

Glory be to thee, O God the Holy Ghost, who, by the finger of thine Almighty power, hast turned about my heart from sin to God.

O great Jehovah, the Lord God Omnipotent, Father, Son, and Holy Ghost, thou art now become my covenant-friend, and I, through thine infinite grace, have become thy covenant-servant. Amen. And the covenant which I have made on earth, let it be ratified in heaven.

[The Minister may here conclude with singing and extemporaneous prayer.]

This covenant we advise you to make, not only in heart, but in word; not only in word, but in writing; and that you would, with all possible reverence, spread the writing before the Lord, as if you would present it to him as your act and deed; and when you have done this, set your hand to it; keep it as a memorial of the solemn transactions that have passed between God and you, and that you may have recourse to it in doubts and temptations.

Section VIII.

FORM FOR LAYING THE CORNER-STONE OF A CHURCH.

The Minister, standing near the place where the stone is to be laid, shall say unto the Congregation:

DEARLY BELOVED, We are taught in the word of God, that, although the heaven of heavens cannot contain the Eternal One, much less the walls of temples made with hands, yet his delight is ever with the sons of men, and that, wherever two or three are gathered in His name, there is He in the midst of them. In all ages His servants have separated certain places for His worship; Jacob erected a stone in Bethel for God's house; Moses made a tabernacle in the desert; and Solomon builded a temple for the Lord, which He filled with the glory of His presence before all the people. We are now assembled to lay the corner-stone of a new house for the worship of the God of our fathers. Let us not doubt that He will favourably approve our godly purpose, and let us now devoutly unite in singing His praise, and in prayer for His blessing on our undertaking.

Let an appropriate Hymn be sung.

Then shall the Minister say:

Let us pray.

Most Glorious God, heaven is Thy throne and the earth is Thy footstool: what house then can be builded for Thee, or where is the place of Thy rest? Yet, blessed be Thy name, O Lord God, that it hath pleased Thee to have Thy habitation among the sons of men, and to dwell in the midst of the assembly of the saints upon the earth. And now, especially, we render thanks unto Thee, O God, that it hath pleased Thee to put it into the hearts of Thy servants to erect in this place a house for Thy worship. We thank Thee for Thy grace which has inclined them to contribute of their substance for the glory of Thy Name: and we pray Thee, to continue Thy blessing upon their pious undertaking. *Amen.*

May many unite with them in their holy work, until this habitation of Thy house shall be completed, and ready for dedication to Thy service, free from all debt or claim of man. *Amen.*

May peace and harmony prevail in the counsels of Thy servants. May the work of this building be accomplished without hurt or accident to any person. And when Thou shalt have prospered the work of their hands upon them, and this house shall be prepared for Thy service, grant that all who shall enjoy the benefit of this pious work, may show forth their thankfulness, by making a right use of it, to the glory of Thy blessed Name ; through Jesus Christ our Lord. *Amen.*

Grant that all who shall hereafter worship Thee in the temple here to be builded, may so serve and please Thee in all holy exercises of godliness, that in the end they may come to the holy place, made without hands, whose builder and maker is God. *Amen.*

Hear us, O Lord, for Thou art our God in whom we trust. And when we shall cease to pray unto Thee on earth, may we, with all those who in like manner have erected such places to Thy name, and with all Thy glorified saints, eternally praise Thee for all Thy goodness vouchsafed unto us on earth and laid up for us in heaven. *Amen.*

Accept these our prayers, we beseech Thee, for the sake of Thy dear Son, who has taught us when we pray to say, " Our Father which art in heaven, Hallowed be thy name, Thy kingdom come. Thy will be done on earth as it is in heaven. Give us this day our daily bread. And forgive us our trespasses, as we forgive them that trespass against us. And lead us not into temptation, but deliver us from evil." *Amen.*

Then shall the Minister read the following Psalm, or the Minister and people may read it in alternate verses; the parts in italics to be read by the people.

Psalm cxxxii.

Lord, remember David, and all his afflictions :

How he sware unto the Lord, and vowed unto the mighty God of Jacob;

Surely I will not come into the tabernacle of my house, nor go up into my bed ;

I will not give sleep to mine eyes, or slumber to mine eyelids,

Until I find out a place for the Lord,

A habitation for the mighty God of Jacob.

Lo, we heard of it at Ephratah : we found it in the fields of the wood.

We will go into his tabernacles : we will worship at his footstool.

Arise, O Lord, into thy rest ; thou, and the ark of thy strength.

Let thy priests be clothed with righteousness ;

And let thy saints shout for joy.

For thy servant David's sake turn not away the face of thine anointed.

The Lord hath sworn in truth unto David : he will not turn from it ;

Of the fruit of thy body will I set upon thy throne.

If thy children will keep my covenant and my testimony that I shall teach them, their children shall also sit upon thy throne for evermore.

For the Lord hath chosen Zion; he hath desired it for his habitation.

This is my rest forever; here will I dwell; for I have desired it.

I will abundantly bless her provision:
I will satisfy her poor with bread.
I will clothe her priests with salvation:
And her saints shall shout aloud for joy.
There will I make the horn of David to bud:
I have ordained a lamp for mine anointed.
His enemies will I clothe with shame:
But upon himself shall his crown flourish.

The Lesson. 1 Cor. iii. 9-23.

For we are labourers together with God: ye are God's husbandry, ye are God's building. According to the grace of God which is given unto me, as a wise master-builder, I have laid the foundation, and another buildeth thereon. But let every man take heed how he buildeth thereupon. For other foundation can no man lay than that is laid, which is Jesus Christ. Now if any man build upon this foundation gold, silver, precious stones, wood, hay, stubble; every man's work shall be made manifest: for the day shall declare it, because it shall be revealed by fire; and the fire shall try every man's work of what sort it is. If any man's work abide which he hath built thereupon, he shall receive a reward. If any man's work shall be burned, he shall suffer loss: but he himself shall be saved; yet so as by fire. Know ye not that ye are the temple of God, and that the Spirit of God dwelleth in you! If any man defile the temple of God, him shall God destroy: for the temple of God is holy, which temple ye are. Let no man deceive himself. If any man among you seemeth to be wise in this world, let him become a fool, that he may be wise. For the wisdom of this world is foolishness with God. For it is written, He taketh the wise in their own craftiness. And again, the Lord knoweth the thoughts of the wise, that they are vain. Therefore let no man glory in men. For all things are yours; whether Paul, or Apollos, or Cephas, or the world, or life, or death, or things present, or things to come; all are yours; and ye are Christ's; and Christ is God's.

Then shall follow the Sermon, or an Address suitable to the occasion, after which the contributions of the people shall be received.

Then shall the Minister, standing by the stone, exhibit to the congregation a vessel to be placed in an excavation of the stone. [It may contain a copy of the Bible, the Hymn Book, the Discipline, Church periodicals of recent date, the names of the Pastor, Trustees, and Building Committee of the Church, with such other documents and articles as may be desired. A list of these may be read.] *After which the person thereto appointed shall deposit the vessel in the stone and cover it; and shall lay the stone, assisted by the builder, saying:*

In the name of the Father, and of the Son, and of the Holy Ghost, I lay this corner-stone for the foundation of a house to be builded and consecrated to the service of Almighty God, according to the order and usages of the Wesleyan Methodist Church. *Amen.*

The service may conclude with extempore prayer, the Lord's Prayer, and the Benediction.

Section IX.

FORM FOR THE DEDICATION OF A CHURCH.

The Congregation being assembled in the Church, the Minister shall say:

DEARLY BELOVED, The Scriptures teach us that God is well pleased with those who build Temples to His name. We have heard how He filled the Temple of Solomon with His glory, and how in the Second Temple He manifested Himself still more gloriously. Let us not doubt that He will approve our purpose of dedicating this house for the performance of the several offices of religious worship; and let us now devoutly join in praise to Almighty God that this godly undertaking hath been so far completed; and in prayer for His further blessing upon all who have been engaged therein, and upon all who shall hereafter worship in this place.

Let an appropriate Hymn be sung, and extemporary prayer be offered, the congregation all kneeling during the prayer.

Then shall the Minister, or some one appointed by him, read

The First Lesson. 2 Chron. vi. 1, 2, 18-21, 40-42; vii. 1-4.

Then said Solomon, The Lord hath said that he would dwell in the thick darkness. But I have built a house of habitation for thee, and a place for thy dwelling forever.

But will God in very deed dwell with men on the earth? Behold heaven and the heaven of heavens cannot contain thee, how much less this house which I have built! Have respect, therefore, to the prayer of thy servant, and to his supplication, O Lord my God, to hearken unto the cry and the prayer which thy servant prayeth before thee: that thine eyes may be open upon this house day and night, upon the place whereof thou hast said thou wouldest put thy name there; to hearken unto the prayer which thy servant prayeth toward this place. Hearken, therefore, unto the supplications of thy servant, and of thy people Israel, which they shall make toward this place, hear them from thy dwelling place, even from heaven; and when thou hearest, forgive.

Now, my God, let, I beseech thee, thine eyes be open, and let thine ears be attent unto the prayer that is made in this place. Now, therefore, arise, O Lord God, into thy resting place, thou, and the ark of thy strength: let thy priests, O Lord God, be clothed with salvation, and let thy saints rejoice in goodness. O Lord God, turn not away the face of thine anointed; remember the mercies of David thy servant.

Now when Solomon had made an end of praying, the fire came down from heaven, and consumed the burnt-offering and the sacrifices; and the glory of the Lord filled the house. And the priests could not enter into the house of the Lord, because the glory of the Lord had filled the Lord's house. And when all the children of Israel saw how the fire came down, and the glory of the Lord upon the house, they bowed themselves with their faces to the ground upon the pavement, and worshipped, and praised the Lord, saying, For he is good; for his mercy endureth forever. Then the king and all the people offered sacrifices before the Lord.

The Second Lesson. Heb. x. 19-26.

Having therefore, brethren, boldness to enter into the holiest by the blood of Jesus, by a new and living way, which he hath consecrated for us, through the veil, that is to say, his flesh; and having a High Priest over the house of God; let us draw near with a true heart in full assurance of faith, having our hearts sprinkled from an evil conscience, and our bodies washed with pure water. Let us hold fast the profession of our faith without wavering; (for he is faithful that promised;) and let us consider one another to provoke unto love and good works; not forsaking the assembling of ourselves together, as the manner of some is; but exhorting one another; and so much the more, as ye see the day approaching. For if we sin wilfully after that we have received the knowledge of the truth, there remaineth no more sacrifice for sins.

Then shall a Hymn be sung, after which the Minister shall deliver a Sermon suitable to the occasion, and after the Sermon the contributions of the people shall be received.

Then shall the Minister read the following Psalm, or the Minister and the Congregation shall read it alternately; the parts in italics to be read by the Congregation.

Psalm cxxii.

I was glad when they said unto me, Let us go into the house of the Lord.

Our feet shall stand within thy gates, O Jerusalem.

Jerusalem is builded as a city that is compact together.

Whither the tribes go up, the tribes of the Lord,

Unto the testimony of Israel, to give thanks unto the name of the Lord.

For there are set thrones of judgment, the thrones of the house of David.

Pray for the peace of Jerusalem:

They shall prosper that love thee.

Peace be within thy walls,
And prosperity within thy palaces.

For my brethren and companions' sakes, I will now say, Peace be within thee.

Because of the house of the Lord our God I will seek thy good.

Then let the Trustees stand up before the Minister, and one of them, or some one in their behalf, say unto him:

We present unto you this building, to be dedicated as a Church for the worship and service of Almighty God.

Then shall the Minister request the Congregation to stand, while he repeats the following

DECLARATION.

DEARLY BELOVED, It is meet and right, as we learn from the Holy Scriptures, that houses erected for the public worship of God should be specially set apart and dedicated to religious uses. For such a dedication we are now assembled. With gratitude, therefore, to Almighty God, who has signally blessed his servants in their holy undertaking to erect this Church, we dedicate it to His service, for the reading of the Holy Scriptures, the preaching of the Word of God, the administration of the Holy Sacraments, and for all other exercises of religious worship and service, according to the Discipline and usages of the Wesleyan Methodist Church. And, as the dedication of the temple is vain without the solemn consecration of the worshippers also, I now call upon you all to dedicate yourselves anew to the service of God. To Him let our souls be dedicated, that they may be renewed after the image of Christ. To Him let our bodies be dedicated, that they may be fit temples for the indwelling of the Holy Ghost. To Him let our labours and business be dedicated, that their fruit may tend to the glory of His great name, and to the advancement of His kingdom. And that he may graciously accept this our solemn act, let us pray.

The Congregation kneeling, the Minister shall offer the following prayer:

O most glorious Lord, we acknowledge that we are not worthy to offer unto thee anything belonging unto us; yet we beseech thee, in thy great goodness, graciously to accept the Dedication of this place to thy service, and to prosper this the work of our hands; receive the prayers and intercessions of all thy servants who shall call upon thee in this house; and give them grace to prepare their hearts to serve thee with reverence and godly fear; affect them with an awful apprehension of thy Divine Majesty, and a deep sense of their own unworthiness; that so approaching thy sanctuary with lowliness and devotion, and coming before thee with pure hearts, bodies undefiled, and minds sanctified, they may always perform a service acceptable to thee; through Jesus Christ our Lord. *Amen.*

Regard, O Lord, the supplications of thy servants, and grant that whosoever shall be dedicated to thee in this house by Baptism, may be found at last in the number of thy faithful children. *Amen.*

Grant, O Lord, that whosoever shall receive in this place the blessed Sacrament of the body and blood of Christ, may come to that holy ordinance with true repentance, faith and charity; and being filled with thy grace and heavenly benediction, may obtain remission of their sins, and all other benefits of his death. *Amen.*

Grant, O Lord, that by thy holy Word, read and preached

in this place, and by the Holy Spirit grafting it inwardly in the heart, the hearers thereof may perceive and know what things they ought to do, and may receive power to perform the same. *Amen.*

Now, therefore, arise, O Lord, and come unto this place of thy rest, thou and the ark of thy strength. Let thine eye be open toward this house day and night; and let thine ears be attent to the prayers of thy children, which they shall offer unto thee in this place: and do thou hear them from heaven, thy dwelling-place, and when thou hearest, forgive. O Lord, we beseech thee, that here and elsewhere thy ministers may be clothed with righteousness and thy saints rejoice in thy salvation. And may we all, with thy people everywhere, grow up into a holy temple in the Lord, and be at last received into the house not made with hands, eternal in the heavens. And to the Father, the Son, and the Holy Spirit, be glory and praise, world without end. *Amen.*

The services may conclude with the Doxology and the Benediction.

CHAPTER VIII.

ON THE CONSTITUTION OF THE FUNDS AND COMMITTEES OF CONNEXIONAL SOCIETIES.

Section I.

THE BOOK AND PRINTING ESTABLISHMENT.

1. What are the regulations for conducting the Book and Printing Establishment?

Ans. The Book and Printing Establishment of the Conference shall be managed by a Book-Steward, under the direction of a Committee, to be nominated by the President, and appointed by the Conference.

2. The Committee shall meet ordinarily for the transaction of business *once a quarter*, viz., on the first Wednesday in August, November, February, and May, or at such other time or times as it may direct; unless in the judgment of the President of the Conference, or of the Book-Steward and Editor, it may be deemed advisable at any time to hold the quarterly meeting on some other day, in which case the members shall be duly notified of the time and place of such meeting. The Book-Steward and Editor, or the

President of Conference, shall have authority to call an extra meeting at any time when in their judgment the interests of the Establishment may require it.

3. The Committee shall make themselves thoroughly acquainted with the position and operations of the Establishment, for which purpose they shall have access to its books, accounts, and apartments. They shall decide the amount of support for Book-Steward and Editor, and quarterly examine the cash and credit sales, as well as the total amount of cash received and expended by the Book-Steward. They shall also have the power, in connection with the President, or Co-Delegate, and Secretary of Conference, to suspend either the Book-Steward or the Editor for incompetency, or for general neglect of duty, and to supply the place so vacated until the ensuing Conference.

4. They shall annually appoint suitable persons to examine the books and audit the accounts of the Book-keeper, and at their last quarterly meeting they shall carefully review the entire operations of the year, and prepare a clear and full Report of the state of the Establishment, to be laid before the Conference. At the end of every four years they shall cause a correct valuation of the stock, machinery, debts, and other property in the possession of the Book-Steward to be made, entering such property at its real saleable value, and the valuation so made shall form the basis of all reports until the next valuation, provided always that in no case shall the Books purchased by the Book-Steward be taken in stock above the real cost of the same when first put into the Stock Room.

5. A Book-Steward shall be appointed by the Conference, who shall hold office for three years, and on entering upon his office a faithful valuation and inventory of all the

property shall be made, when the entire amount so valued shall be confided to his care. It shall be his duty to purchase the materials and goods required for the Establishment, keeping in view the general wants of the Connexion, and the religious instruction of the people. But he shall publish no book at the expense of the Conference without the consent of the Book Committee. He shall give the Committee such information as they may require concerning the business of the Establishment. He shall annually present to the Conference a balance-sheet exhibiting the financial state of the concern, together with an abstract of the cash account, showing the sources whence the money has been received, and the purposes for which paid. He shall conduct the business of the Establishment in the most economical and efficient manner, and shall pay over from time to time to the Treasurer of the *Superannuation Fund* such portion of the profits as the Committee may deem consistent with the best interests of the Book Room.

6. An Editor shall be annually appointed by the Conference, who, in the editorial management of the *Christian Guardian* and other publications committed to his care, shall act in concurrence with the judgment of the Committee. It shall be his duty to make the *Christian Guardian* as instructive and interesting as possible, and to see that all books and periodicals published by the Book Room are carefully printed. In all matters touching the publication of the *Guardian*, it is expected that the Book Steward and Editor will act in harmony.

Concerning the Sale of Books.

7. No Minister or Preacher shall sell, or publish for sale, any books but such as are sent regularly from our Book Room.

Every Minister or Preacher is peremptorily required finally to settle his book account for the preceding year at each Conference; and also regularly to transmit the money in his hands, without any reservation or deduction whatever, to the Book-Steward, whenever it shall amount to ten dollars. Should any Minister or Preacher, having claims on the Connexional Funds, fail to pay up his account with the office as above directed, it shall be the duty of the Book-Steward, annually, to draw upon the Treasurer of any of those funds, an amount not exceeding one-fourth of the claim of the Brother on such fund, towards the payment of his debt; and the Treasurer of each fund is hereby directed to honour such drafts when presented.

SECTION II.

SUPERANNUATED MINISTERS' FUND.

This Fund was incorporated in 1851 by an Act of the Provincial Parliament, under the name of " The Connexional Society of the Wesleyan Methodist Church in Canada." 14th and 15th Vic., cap. 142.

Constitution of the Board of Management.

1. This Fund shall be managed by a Central Board, consisting of eight members of the Conference, and a Treasurer, (who shall be *ex-officio* a member of the Central Board,) who shall be appointed by the Conference upon the nomination of the President.

2. The members of the Central Board shall be elected for a term of three years, one-third of whom shall retire annually, but shall, nevertheless, be eligible for re-election.

3. The Central Board for the year 1863, shall consist of the Reverends Anson Green, D.D., Asahel Hurlburt, Thomas Cosford, Richard Jones, Samuel Rose, and John Douse, Treasurer.

The Fund.

This Fund shall consist of the annual income arising—

1. From the interest of such moneys as are invested in its behalf.

2. From subscriptions and donations taken up annually in the Classes and among the lay friends of the Church, during the months of November and December. The amount to be remitted to the Treasurer on or before the first day of January in each year.

3. From the annual subscriptions of all our Travelling Ministers and Preachers, which shall not be less than five dollars each, to be paid to the Financial Secretary at the May District Meeting, and by him remitted to the Treasurer of the Superannuated Ministers' Fund, not later than the *first day* of each Conference.

4. From such moneys as may be appropriated from the profits of the Book and Printing Establishment.

Miscellaneous Regulations.

1. The period for computing Ministers' claims on the Superannuated Ministers' Fund shall commence from the time of their being received by the Conference *for our work*, except such Preachers as were employed previously to the November Quarterly Meeting, under the direction of a Chairman of a District, to whom the whole year shall be allowed.

2. All Ministers hereafter coming to us from other Churches, or other branches of the Wesleyan Church, shall be allowed a claim upon the Fund, according to the number of years they shall have travelled in connexion with *our Conference*, and on payment of such sums as may be deemed equitable by the Conference.

3. All those lay-members and friends who have paid one pound or upwards annually to the Fund, shall have their names printed in the Minutes of Conference; and shall be entitled to receive a copy of the Annual Minutes gratis.

4. When Superannuated Ministers are authorized by their District Meetings to attend Conference, their travelling expenses shall be allowed them.

SECTION III.

THE CONTINGENT FUND.

Art. 1. This Fund, denominated "The Contingent Fund of the Wesleyan Methodist Church in Canada," is established for the purpose of aiding those Circuits which have not been able to pay their Ministers' or Preachers' Salaries; for relieving cases of special affliction, and for defraying extraordinary expenses incurred in the service of the Church.

Art. 2. In addition to the amount granted by the English Conference, there shall be public collections made in all our congregations during the months of September and March in each year.

Art. 3. The Committee of the Contingent Fund shall consist of Thirty Members—namely, Fifteen Ministers appointed by the Conference, and an equal number of Laymen chosen by the Recording Stewards and Lay Representatives at the May District Meetings of several Districts most contiguous to the place of holding the ensuing Conference, such Districts to be named by the preceding Conference.

Art. 4. The Committee shall meet annually at the place of holding the Conference, on the First Tuesday of the Conference, at 7 o'clock, p.m.

Art. 5. The Committee shall appoint annually from among themselves, a Chairman, Secretary, Treasurer and two Auditors.

1. It shall be the duty of the Secretary to keep a book in which shall be inserted the Constitution and By-Laws, and in which he shall keep a record of the proceedings of all the meetings of the Committee; and to sign all orders upon the Treasurer which have been authorized by the Committee.

2. It shall be the duty of the Treasurer to receive all moneys, and make such disbursements as have been authorized by the Committee and signed by the Secretary, and to render to the Committee an annual detailed account of the same.

3. It shall be the duty of the Auditors to examine the accounts of the Treasurer annually, and present their Report to the Committee.

Art. 6. All applications for grants from this Fund shall be presented to the Committee by the Chairman of the District from which the claim is made, or by such other person as he may appoint to represent his District.

Art. 7. No application for special or additional grants to any Circuit shall be entertained by this Committee, unless such Circuit has raised during each quarter the average sum of fifty cents per member.

Art. 8. No application for additional aid to Circuits, or special claims, shall be entertained by this Committee unless they have passed the Quarterly Meeting, and have been signed by the Recording Steward, and recommended by the District Meeting.

Art. 9. All applications for expenses incurred in the general work, or for other claims not otherwise specified, shall be submitted to the Committee in detail for their investigation and approval.

Art. 10. A Financial District Meeting, consisting of the Superintendents of Circuits and Missions and one Steward from each Circuit and Mission, shall be held in each District in the month of September, in which the sum granted to that District by the Committee shall be apportioned to the different Circuits as fairly and impartially as possible.

Art. 11. Any Circuit which in the past year has received assistance from the Contingent Fund, may or may not obtain aid the next year, as the Financial District Meeting may see fit; even though the said Circuit may or may not have been considered in the appropriation made to the District by this Committee.

Art. 12. One half of the amounts granted by the Committee to each District shall be forwarded by the Treasurer to the Financial Secretary of such District in the month of December, and the balance paid over to him during the first week of Conference.

Art. 13. The collections taken up for this Fund in September and March shall be paid over by Superintendents to the Financial Secretaries of their several Districts not later than the 15th of the following months respectively.

Section II.

THE CHILDREN'S FUND.

1. This Fund shall be denominated "The Children's Fund of the Wesleyan Methodist Church in Canada," and

is established for the purpose of providing more effectively and uniformly for the payment of the Disciplinary allowances of the Children of our Ministers, and of equalizing the claims for this object on the several Circuits of our work.

The Committee.

The Committee for the management of this Fund shall be composed of all the Financial Secretaries; together with a General Treasurer and a General Secretary, to be annually nominated by the Committee, and appointed by the Conference.

The Committee shall meet annually at the place of holding the Conference, one day previous to its commencement, and at such other times as may be deemed necessary.

It shall be the duty of the Committee:

1. To appoint annually a Chairman to preside at its meetings.

2. To appoint annually two Auditors to examine the accounts of the Treasurer, and report to the Committee.

3. To ascertain the amount requisite to meet the claims upon this Fund, and the average amount required from each member of the Church for this purpose. The number of members being taken from the official returns made to the Conference.

4. To prepare an annual report of the state of the Fund, which, with the Treasurer's Report, shall be published in the Minutes of Conference.

The Income.

1. The Income of this Fund shall be raised upon the several Circuits and Missions, according to a rate recommended by the Committee, and approved by the Conference;

and this amount *shall be the first claim* upon the income of each Circuit and Mission ; and when the amount due by any Circuit or Mission to this Fund, shall exceed the claim of such Circuit or Mission upon the Fund, the Recording Steward shall remit the balance (quarterly) to the Financial Secretary of his District ; and when the Financial Secretary has a balance in his hands, after paying the claims of the several Circuits of his District, he shall forward the same to the General Treasurer, who shall distribute it to the several Districts according to their respective claims.

2. The number of members for which each Circuit or District shall be responsible, shall be that returned to the previous Conference ; with such alterations only as are caused by the change of boundaries previously sanctioned by the Conference.

3. The Book and Printing Establishment, Colleges, and other Connexional Institutions, shall respectively pay to the Treasurer of this Fund the amounts due to the Ministers connected with such Institutions for their Children's allowances, and such Ministers shall receive their allowances for their children from the said Treasurer.

The Claimants.

1. The regular claimants upon this fund, are such children of Ministers engaged in the active work as were born after their fathers had been received into full connexion with the Conference.

2. Each Superannuated Minister shall receive from the Children's Fund for each child under eighteen years of age —if not otherwise provided for—the sum of one dollar annually for each year that he has been employed in the effective work in our Conference : Provided always, that he

does not receive more than the sum of thirty dollars for each child.

3. All Superannuated Ministers who shall have been employed *less than fifteen years* in the effective work, shall receive the amount to which they are entitled according to the above scale, *for four years* after the time of their superannuation, when their claim on the Fund shall cease: Provided always, that all Superannuated Ministers shall receive the full amount of thirty dollars for each child for *two years* after their superannuation, without respect to the above rule.

The children of *Deceased Ministers* are entitled to the same claims as those of Superannuated Ministers.

4. The maximum sum for each member of the Church to pay into this fund shall not exceed thirty-five cents; and when the sum thus collected shall not pay the several claimants according to the Discipline, then each claimant shall receive an amount proportioned to his claim up to the full amount of the current income.

5. The Financial Secretaries shall be the Treasurers of the Children's Fund for their respective Districts, and shall make a correct record in their District books at each May District Meeting, of the names, ages, and dates of birth of each claimant upon the fund for whom payment is made; a similar record of those whose claims are prospective for the ensuing year; the number of members on each Circuit for the past year, and the number of members to be reported to the ensuing Conference.

A schedule, containing suitable columns for these records, shall be furnished by the Treasurer, and filled by the Financial Secretary, and handed to the Treasurer the day previous to the opening of the Conference.

6. The Financial Secretary shall not, at the May District Meeting, place upon the list of prospective claimants the name of any child born after the fifteenth of May then current; nor shall any such child be included in the estimates for the ensuing year, nor be paid for by any Treasurer; nor will the claim of any child be admitted whose name was not reported to the Financial Secretary at the previous May District Meeting.

7. Each Minister, having children claimants upon this Fund, shall, at the Financial District Meeting, furnish the Financial Secretary with a list of their names and ages, counting to the fifteenth of May previous.

Section III.

CHURCH RELIEF FUND.

1. This Fund, denominated "THE CHURCH RELIEF FUND *of the Wesleyan Methodist Church in Canada*," is established for the purpose of aiding such Churches as are deeply involved in debt, and greatly needing assistance.

2. All Churches applying for assistance must be regularly deeded, and *legally secured* to the Connexion by being *registered* according to law, within one year after possession.

3. No application for assistance from the Church Relief Fund will be entertained unless the Trustees of the Church for which the application is made *subscribe at least one dollar each to the General Fund*, and pledge themselves to raise an amount at least *equal to the sum granted from the Fund;* nor will any sum be appropriated or paid by the Treasurer of the Fund until a statement duly authenticated

be furnished that the sum raised by local effort has been collected for the purposes specified.

4. No District shall have any claims on the Church Relief Fund until the Financial Secretary of such District has made a return of the money to the General Treasurer. The Financial Secretaries are required to make these returns on or before the first day of the Conference.

5. The Committee of the Church Relief Fund shall consist of one Minister from each District, to be appointed by the May District Meeting, and twenty-one laymen, to be appointed by the same authority as those appointing the Contingent Fund Committee, from the several Districts most contiguous to the place of holding the ensuing Conference,—such Districts and their proportion to be named by the preceding Conference.

6. This Committee shall meet during the sessions of each Conference, when all applications must be considered by them. And the particular state of each Church requiring relief, as to debts and resources, or income and expenditure, &c., shall be laid before the Committee *in writing*.

7. This Fund shall consist of: 1. *Public Collections* in all our Churches and Congregations, to be made annually during the month of July. 2. *Subscriptions of Trustees*, of one dollar or upwards, annually. 3. Such *Legacies* as may be bequeathed by members or friends of the Church. The amount collected and subscribed shall be paid without fail to the Financial Secretaries, at the Financial District Meeting, and by them forthwith transmitted to the General Treasurer.

8. The moneys which are thus raised shall be annually appropriated by the Church Relief Fund Committee, at each Conference, for the relief of such Churches as are involved in debt and greatly need assistance.

9. The Committee shall appoint a Chairman, a Secretary, and two Auditors—the Treasurer shall be appointed by the Conference.

10. All the business of the Committee shall be annually reported to the Conference, and subject to its sanction.

Section IV.

EDUCATIONAL FUND.

FOR THE EDUCATION OF CANDIDATES FOR THE MINISTRY.

1. The Conference, by a direct vote, shall appoint such young men to attend Victoria College as it may deem proper.

2. Those only shall be sent by Conference, in connection with the Educational Fund, whose circumstances require that their expenses, in whole or in part, shall be met by that Fund.

3. Before any Candidate, who may desire to go to our College, shall be sent there, his circumstances shall be inquired into by the District Meeting; and in the event of his being appointed to go to College by the Conference, the District Meeting minute of his circumstances shall be forwarded by the Secretary to the Chairman of the Educational Fund Committee. Nevertheless, no Candidate for our Ministry shall be sent to College who has not travelled at least one year in our work.

4. The Educational Fund Committee shall consist of ten persons: one half to be Ministers appointed by the Confer-

ence, and one half to be Laymen appointed by the District Meeting in whose bounds the Conference shall be held. The election of lay representatives to this fund shall be subject to the same rule as that which directs like elections to the other Funds of our Connexion.

5. This Committee shall elect from among themselves a Secretary, a Treasurer, and two Auditors.

6. The Committee shall have power to apportion the funds raised in behalf of the Educational Fund for those young men who are appointed by the Conference to attend College, as they shall judge expedient.

7. They shall present annually to the Conference, for publication in the Minutes, a report of all moneys received and expended.

Section V.

REVISED CONSTITUTION OF THE MISSIONARY SOCIETY OF THE W. M. CHURCH IN CANADA.

ARTICLE 1. This Institution shall be designated the "Wesleyan Methodist Auxiliary Missionary Society in Canada."

2. The object of this Society is to excite and combine, in a plan more systematic and efficient than has been heretofore accomplished, the exertions of the societies and congregations (and others who are friends to the conversion of the heathen and the extension of the Gospel) in the support and enlargement of the Indian and Domestic Missions, which are carried on under the sanction and direction of the Conference of the Wesleyan Methodist Church in Canada.

3. Every person subscribing and paying annually the sum of four dollars and upwards, and every benefactor pre-

senting a donation of forty dollars and upwards, shall be deemed a member of this Society, and entitled, as such, to a General Annual Report.

4. All Methodist Missionary Societies which have already been formed, or which may be formed, for the several Districts into which the Methodist Connexion is divided, shall be entitled "Auxiliary Methodist Missionary Societies" for the District in which they have been, or may be formed. All Methodist Missionary Societies already formed, or hereafter to be formed, in the particular Circuits of any district, shall be entitled "Branch Methodist Missionary Societies" for the Circuits in which they are or shall be established. And Sabbath School and Juvenile Christmas Offerings are also earnestly recommended, where exertions of that nature are likely to be advantageous.

5. The Chairman of each District shall be, *ex-officio*, Secretary and Treasurer of the Auxiliary Society of his District: and every Superintendent of a Circuit shall, by virtue of his office, be Secretary and Treasurer of the Branch Societies of the Circuit over which he presides.

6. The money raised in any Circuit for the Methodist Missions by Branch Societies, or other local Associations, and all other money, in whatever way collected for the same object, shall be regularly paid once every half year, or oftener, into the hands of the Treasurer of the Auxiliary Society for the District in which the said Circuit is situated, with the deduction only of such sums as may have been disbursed for the incidental and local expenses of the Branch Society. And the Treasurer of every District Society shall remit to the Treasurer of the General Society in Toronto, semi-annually or oftener, all sums so received by him from the various Circuits in his District, deducting only there-

from the necessary incidental expenses incurred by the Auxiliary Society.

7. The Secretaries of every Branch Society, or other local association, shall forward annually to the Secretary of the Auxiliary Society of their District, a list of all the benefactors and subscribers during the preceding twelve months, with an account of their respective contributions. And the Secretaries of every District Auxiliary Society shall also forward annually to the Secretary of the General Society in Toronto a similar list of all the subscribers and benefactors in all the Circuits of their Districts, an abstract of the accounts of the Auxiliary Society, showing its gross receipts, its local payments, and its remittances to the General Treasurer.

8. All benefactors of forty dollars and upwards, and all subscribers of one pound and upwards annually to any of the Auxiliary or Branch Societies in connection with this Institution shall be deemed, in right of such benefaction or subscription, members of the General Society.

9. All persons who collect to the amount of twelve dollars and upwards annually for this Institution, or for any of the Auxiliaries, Branches, or Associations, shall also be members of the General Society, and entitled to receive a copy of the Annual Report.

10. An annual public meeting of the members and friends of this Society, at such time and connected with such religious service as may be deemed expedient, shall be held at the place appointed by the committee. At this annual meeting the officers of the Society shall be appointed.

11. A General Committee shall be annually appointed by the Conference, to whom shall be entrusted (in the intervals of the annual assemblies of that body) the superinten-

dence of the collection and disbursements of all money received for the Missions which are now, or may hereafter be carried on under its sanction, and by the Ministers in connection with it. The Committee shall consist of the President and Secretary of the Conference for the time being, the Co-Delegate, the General Secretaries of Missions, the Chairmen of Districts, and not less than seven other Ministers, nor more than the entire number of Chairmen, to be nominated by the President, and elected by the Conference, who, together with an equal number of laymen, shall possess and exercise all the powers now employed by the Missionary Committee and Board.

12. Each District Meeting, when the Stewards are present, shall elect one layman, as a member of this Committee, and the Conference shall appoint the remaining number in the same way in which the Ministers of the Committee are appointed.

13. The Chairmen shall require regular quarterly communications to be made by each of the Missionaries on their respective Districts to the Corresponding Secretary of the Society, giving information of the state and prospects of the several missions in which they are employed.

14. It shall be the duty of the General Missionary Committee to furnish the General Treasurer of the Society with a schedule setting forth the number of missions and mission schools, the place of location and the amount appropriated for their support respectively, and the sum total of appropriation for the current year.

15. This Constitution shall not be altered but by a general meeting of the Society, on the recommendation of the Conference and Committee.

CHAPTER IX.

ARTICLES OF UNION BETWEEN THE BRITISH WESLEYAN METHODIST CONFERENCE

AND THE

CONFERENCE OF THE WESLEYAN METHODIST CHURCH IN CANADA.

I. That the Conference and Connexion of Western Canada be placed in such union with the British Conference, as nearly as local and other circumstances will allow, as that which the Conference and Connexion in Ireland now sustain to the latter body :

The Chapels and other property now held in trust for the Wesleyan Church in Canada, remain exclusively under the control of the Conference, known in law as "The Conference of the Wesleyan Methodist Church in Canada."

II. That the British Conference shall annually appoint one of their number, or a member of our Body, as President of the Canadian Conference, and a second Minister as an Associate of the President so appointed, and his Co-Delegate, from the said British Conference, who may be either a British or a Canadian Minister, in full connexion with either Conference, as may from time to time be judged most convenient. If the appointed President cannot remain in Canada during the whole year of his Presidency, his Associate and Co-Delegate shall for the remainder of that year take his place in Canada, in order to superintend generally, in connection with the regular authorities there, the work of God, and to promote the great objects of the Reunion now contemplated. In the event of the English Conference not appointing a President, or the President appointed not arriving in Canada, the Canada Conference shall appoint a President, who shall appoint his own Co-Delegate.

III. That in accordance with the preceding Resolution, by which it is provided that the future relation of the Canada Conference to the British Conference shall be, as nearly as may be, similar to that which is now sustained with the British Conference by the Conference and Connexion in Ireland, all and every the acts, admissions, expulsions and appointments whatsoever of the Canadian Conference, the same being put into writing, and signed by the President, or by the Minister appointed as his Associate and Co-Delegate, shall be annually laid before the ensuing British Conference, and when confirmed by their vote, shall be deemed, taken, and be, to all intents and purposes, valid and obligatory, from the respective times when the same shall have been ordered or done by the said Canadian Conference.

Provided always, that all appointments to Chapels in Canada, the Trusts of which require that the appointment of Ministers and Preachers shall be made by the Canadian Conference, shall be of absolute authority from the time of such appointment by that Conference.

IV. That for the present the existing *Book of Discipline* of the Canadian Conference, shall remain in force, with the exception of such articles as may be affected by any of these proposals for accomplishing the desired Re-Union; subject however, to any improvements or amendments which may hereafter from time to time be mutually agreed upon; and with the impression that in order that the future Union may be complete, cordial, and practically efficient, the Discipline, Economy, and Form of Church Government of the British Connexion shall, as far as possible, (in conformity with the terms of Article II. of the *former agreement in* 1833), be introduced into the Societies in Upper Canada.

General Superintendent.

V. That the British Conference shall appoint a General Superintendent of the Missions, and Mission Schools, in Western Canada, (to act under the direction of the Wesleyan Missionary Committee,) who shall be, ex-officio, a member of the Stationing Committee of the Canada Conference, as well as of the Conference.

VI. That the Missions among the Indian Tribes and new settlers, which are now or may be hereafter established in Canada West, shall be regarded as Missions of the English Wesleyan Missionary Society, under the following Regulations, viz. :—1. That the Parent Committee in London shall determine the amount to be annually applied to the support and extension of Missions; and the sum granted shall be distributed by a Committee consisting of the President and Secretary of Conference, the Co-Delegate, the General Superintendent of Missions, the Chairmen of Districts, and not less than seven other Ministers, nor more than the entire number of Chairmen; to be nominated by the General Superintendent of Missions, and elected by the Conference, who, together with an equal number of laymen, shall possess and exercise all the powers now employed by the Missionary Committee and Board.

Each District Meeting, when the Stewards are present, shall elect one layman as a member of this Committee, and the Conference shall appoint the remaining number in the same way in which the Ministers of the Committee are appointed.

2. That the Methodist Missionary Society in Western Canada, under the sanction of the Conference there, shall be auxiliary to the Wesleyan Missionary Society in London; and that all sums which may be contributed to its funds shall be paid over to the Treasurers of the Wesleyan Missionary Society.

3. That all Missionaries of the Parent Wesleyan Missionary Society now in Canada, shall be stationed by the Canada Conference in the same way as other Preachers of that Conference; but in the appointment of the Missionaries, the General Superintendent of Missions, as well as the Co-Delegate of the President (referred to in a preceding resolution), shall be associated with the President of the Conference and the Chairmen of Districts in their appointment.

4. That the Missionaries who may be in full connection with the British Conference, or any other Missionaries hereafter to be sent, who may be in full connexion with that Conference, shall, notwithstanding the Union between the Canada and the British Conference, so far retain their connexion with the latter as not to lose any claims, privileges, or pecuniary advantages which may belong to them, by virtue of their relation to the British Conference.

5. That the trial of all Missionaries sent to Canada in full connexion with the British Conference, who may at any time be accused of misconduct, or of any deviation from the doctrines and discipline of the Methodist Connexion, shall be left with the District Meetings to which such Missionaries may respectively belong, and subsequently to the Canada Conference; but such Missionaries in full connexion with the British Conference shall have a right of appeal to that Conference.

6. That a joint application be made, on behalf of the Committee of the Wesleyan Missionary Society and the Representatives of the Canadian Conference, to the Imperial and Colonial authorities, that the sum heretofore allowed as a Government Grant in support of Wesleyan Missions in Western Canada, may be paid to the Treasurers of the Wesleyan Missionary Society, to assist that Society in the support and extension of Missions in Canada.

7. That as these arrangements will involve the financial interests of the Wesleyan Missionary Society, this Committee recommend the Wesleyan Missionary Committee to make such allowances, as far as they may be able, to meet the peculiarities of the case, and to assist the Canadian Conference in extending its operations, not only on the present Missionary Stations, but in new and destitute settlements which may be more nearly connected with the regular work; and this Committee indulge the hope that the Missionary Committee will carry out this recommendation in a liberal and generous spirit.

This Committee now appoint a *Sub-Committee*, to prepare a statement of probable Income and Expenditure, as the same may be affected by the Re-Union, and of the probable amount which it may be desirable that the Missionary Committee may be requested to grant; to be laid before the earliest meeting of that Committee.

This Sub-Committee to consist of Messrs. Marsden, Alder, Lord, Richey, and Stinson, who are requested to confer with Messrs. Ryerson and Green on this subject.

VII. That this Committee, in unison with the sentiments expressed by Messrs. Ryerson and Green, entertain a strong conviction that the proposed Re-Union would be greatly facilitated by the early visit of the Rev. Dr. Alder to the Societies and Congregations in Canada, and to attend and preside at the next annual meeting of the Conference; and therefore present their earnest and most respectful request to their esteemed brother, Dr. Alder, that he will kindly undertake this most important mission, in which he will be associated with the prayers and best wishes of the Committee, for his prosperous voyage, continued health, successful exertions, and safe return to this country.

VIII. That the Committee recommend that, for the purpose of effectually carrying out the object contemplated in the above resolutions, a Special District Meeting of the Missionaries of Western Canada shall be summoned, as early as may be convenient, and that Dr. Alder and the Rev. Matthew Richey be respectfully requested to attend the meeting of that District; and the Committee recommend that Dr. Alder should go out on his visit to Canada as early as may be consistent with his personal comfort and official engagement.

IX. That the President of the Conference be requested to send a respectful and affectionate letter to the Conference in Canada, acknowledging the receipt of the Address sent to the Conference in Bristol, stating the appointment, the satisfaction which the Committee have felt in meeting the

Deputation of the Canada Conference, and the earnest hope of the Committee that the measures which they have recommended may tend to promote a permanent and happy Union.

X. That the cordial and respectful thanks of the Committee are due to the Venerated President of the Conference, for the kind and able manner in which he has presided over its deliberations.

(Signed,)
WILLIAM ATHERTON,
*President of the Conference, and
Chairman of the Committee.*

The preceding articles were submitted to the Conference of the Wesleyan Methodist Church in Canada, held in Toronto, on Wednesday, the second day of June, one thousand eight hundred and forty-seven, and fully concurred in.

(Signed,) W. RYERSON, *President.*

ALTERATIONS IN THE FOREGOING ARTICLES OF UNION, AGREED UPON BY THE CANADIAN AND BRITISH CONFERENCES OF 1870.

1. That the following words be substituted for Article V., which provides for the appointment of a General Superintendent of Missions, viz. : "That the Canadian Conference may from time to time appoint a Secretary or Secretaries of the Canadian Wesleyan Missionary Society, who shall be *ex-officio* a member or members of the Stationing Committee."

2. That the first paragraph of Article VI. hereafter read as follows, viz. : "That the Missionary Society of the Wesleyan Methodist Church in Canada shall be regarded as affiliated to the English Wesleyan Missionary Society ;

and the Missions of the Wesleyan Methodist Church in Canada shall be under the direction and control of the Canadian Conference."

3. That clause 2, and all of clause 3 after the words "Preachers of that Conference," shall henceforward be inoperative.

Provided also, that nothing contained in the above alterations in the Articles of Union shall be so construed as to affect the claim of the Canadian Conference upon the continuation of the grant heretofore annually made by the English Conference or Missionary Society to the Contingent Fund of the Canadian Conference.

MODEL DEED.

PREAMBLE.

This Indenture, made the twenty-fourth day of May, in the year of our Lord one thousand eight hundred and fifty, between *Joseph Bloor*, of the village of Yorkville, in the county of York, in the Home District and Province of Canada, Gentleman, of the first part : *Sarah Bloor*, wife of the said Joseph Bloor, of the same place, of the second part ; and *James Wallis*, of the village of Yorkville, aforesaid, Blacksmith ; *George Hazelton White*, of the same place, Builder ; *Joseph Bloor*, of the same place, Gentleman ; *George Revill*, of the same place, Sexton ; *Bartholomew Bull*, of the township of York, Yeoman ; *George Rowell*, of the city of Toronto, Brewer ; *Richard Woodsworth*, of the same place, Builder ; *Richard Yates*, of the same place, Grocer ; and *Richard Hastings*, of the same place, Merchant; members of the Wesleyan Methodist Church in Canada, in connexion with the English Conference, TRUSTEES for the purpose hereinafter set forth, of the third part ;

Whereas in an by an act of Parliament of Upper Canada, passed in the ninth year of the reign of His late Majesty King George the Fourth, entitled "An Act for the Relief of the Religious Societies therein mentioned," it is enacted, that whenever any Religious Congregation or Society of Methodists [and other denominations mentioned in the said Act,] shall have occasion to take a conveyance of Land, for the site of a Church, Meeting-House, or Chapel, or a Burying-Ground, it shall and may be lawful for them to appoint Trustees, to whom, and their successors to be appointed in such manner as shall be specified in the Deed, the requsite land for all or any of the purposes aforesaid, (not exceeding five acres for any one Congregation,) may be conveyed, and such Trustees, and their successors in perpetual succession, by the name expressed in such Deed, shall be capable of taking, holding, and possessing such Land, and of commencing and maintaining any actions in Law or Equity, for the protection thereof and of their right thereto :

And whereas, by a certain other Act of the Parliament of Upper Canada, the assent of Her Majesty whereto was promulgated in this Province in the fifth year of Her Majesty's reign, after in part reciting the above mentioned Act, it is amongst other things enacted, That so much of the said Act as limits the powers of the several denominations mentioned in the said Act to the quantity of Five Acres, and to the purposes for which Lands shall be held, should be, and the same was thereby repealed ; and that the several Religious Societies mentioned in the said Act should and were thereby authorized to hold lands in the manner specified in the said Act for the support of public worship and the propagation of Christian knowledge, as well as for the purposes mentioned in the said Act, anything in the Statutes, commonly called the Statutes of Mortmain, to the contrary nothwithstanding :

And whereas, a Religious Congregation or Society of Methodists have occasion and are desirous to take a conveyance of the Lands and Premises hereby conveyed, for the purposes authorized by the said Acts, and have appointed the Trustees herein above named by the name of the "TRUSTEES OF THE WESLEYAN METHODIST CHURCH IN CANADA," of Yorkville, in the Township of York, in the Home District, and Province of Canada :

And whereas in order the better to understand the intent and meaning of these presents, it is desirable briefly to recite the origin and formation of the said Wesleyan Methodist Church in Canada, in connexion with the English Conference ; (that is to say),

In or about the year one thousand seven hundred and ninety, certain Ministers or Preachers of the Gospel, being members of the New York Conference of the Methodist Episcopal Church in the United States of America, were ordained and sent by the Reverend Francis Asbury, one of the Bishops of said Church, into various parts of Canada, where they preached the Gospel of our Lord Jesus Christ, and united in Classes and Religious Societies, such persons as professed faith in the doctrines taught by the said Ministers or Preachers, and adherence to the Rules and Discipline of the said Methodist Episcopal Church ; and such Classes and Religious Societies continued to increase in number, until in process of time Circuits were duly organized in the said Province, and supplied with the word and ordinances of God by Ministers appointed by Bishops of the said Church :

In or about the year one thousand eight hundred and seventeen, certain Ministers or Preachers of the Gospel were also sent into the said Province, by the Wesleyan Missionary Committee in London, England, being Ministers in connexion with the Conference of " The people called Methodists," in England, as known by a certain Deed Poll or Instrument in writing under the hand and seal of the Reverend John Wesley, (formerly of Lincoln College, Oxford, and

MODEL DEED. 179

afterwards of the City Road, London,) Clerk, bearing date on or about the twenty-eighth day of February, one thousand seven hundred and eighty-four, attested by two credible witnesses, and enrolled in His Majesty's High Court of Chancery, or or about the ninth day of March, in the year last aforesaid ; (which said Conference of the People called Methodists, is otherwise generally known, and is hereinafter called, by the name of "The English Conference :) the said Ministers or Preachers also united in Classes and Religious Societies, divers persons in the said Province as members under the direction and Rules and Government of the said English Conference :

In or about the year one thousand eight hundred and twenty, an arrangement was mutually entered into between the General Conference of the said Methodist Episcopal Church in the United States of America, and the said English Conference, by which the Ministers of the English Conference were to be withdrawn from the Province of Upper Canada ; and the persons under their pastoral care and direction were united with the Societies under the care and direction of the Ministers of the said Methodist Episcopal Church :

In or about the year one thousand eight hundred and twenty-four, arrangements were made for the assembling of a yearly Conference of the said Ministers or Preachers in Canada, called "The Canada Conference," under direction or oversight of a Bishop or Bishops, of the said Methodist Episcopal Church : In the year one thousand eight hundred and twenty-eight, in compliance with a memorial from the said Canada Conference, addressed to the Bishops and Members of the General Conference of the said Methodist Episcopal Church in the United States of America, the Ministers composing the said Conference, were authorized by the said General Conference to form themselves and their Societies under their pastoral care into an independent Church in Canada : And a Church was accordingly constituted, having the style and title of the "Methodist Episcopal Church in Canada ;" Thenceforward, the Ministers of the said Methodist Episcopal Church in Canada, continued to meet together in Conference annually, and in the year one thousand eight hundred and thirty-two, proposals, were made for a Union between the said Conference in Canada and the English Conference, for the purpose of concentrating their joint efforts for the spread of true religion throughout the Province ; And, after mature consideration and negotiation upon the matters involved in the said proposals, Articles of Union were agreed upon by the said English Conference and the Conference of the Methodist Episcopal Church in Canada, and ratified in York, (now the City of Toronto), in Upper Canada, by an instrument in writing, bearing date the second day of October, one thousand eight hundred and thirty-three, and signed on behalf of the said Conference in Canada, by Egerton Ryerson, and on behalf of the said English Conference, by George Marsden : in connexion with the establishment of the said Union, the appointment to the office of Bishop (no Bishop having been ordained in or for the said Church,) was made annual, according to the provisions of the Discipline of said Church, and as contemplated in the said Articles of Union: And also, a change was made in certain portions of the Discipline of the said Church in Canada, in order to assimilate them more nearly to the economy and usages of the Parent Body, under the direction of the English Conference:

In consequence of these arrangements and alterations, the style and title of the said Methodist Episcopal Church in Canada, was changed: and the said Church in Canada was designated, "The Wesleyan Methodist Church in British North America," which style and title was again changed in the year one thousand eight hundred and thirty-four, to that of "The Wesleyan Methodist Church in Canada: Certain misunderstandings which occurred between the English Conference and the said Conference in Canada, in or about the year one thousand eight hundred and forty, occasioned a temporary suspension of the practical operation of the Union, effected as above recited, until in the year one thousand eight hundred and forty-seven, mutual arrangements were made between the said Conference in Canada, and the English Conference, to restore their unanimity of action in carrying on the work of God in the said Province: As the basis of this arrangement, certain Articles of Settlement and Re-Union were agreed upon by the said Conferences; which articles were adopted by the Conference of the Wesleyan Methodist Church in Canada, at their annual meeting begun in Toronto aforesaid, on the second day of June, in the year one thousand eight hundred and forty seven, and which Articles are printed in the Book of Discipline of the said Church:

Now, therefore, the Conference of the Wesleyan Methodist Church in connexion with the English Conferences is and shall be held and taken by these presents to be, for all the intents and purposes herein contained, and for all the intents and purposes of any other deeds and instruments, whether at law or in equity, in which reference shall be made to this Indenture, composed of such ordained Ministers of God's word as now are, and so long as they shall continue to be, in accordance with the Rules and Discipline thereof, members in full connexion with the Conference of the Wesleyan Methodist Church in Canada, and of such ordained Ministers of God's word as now are, and so long as they shall be members in full connexion with the said English Conference, and are appointed to Circuits or Stations, or Offices in Canada, by the said Conference in Canada, and of such ordained Ministers of God's word as shall be from time to time and at all times hereafter admitted into and continued in full connexion with the said Conference in Canada, and of such ordained Ministers of God's word as shall be and continue to be in full connexion with the said English Conference, and shall be appointed to Circuits or Stations, or Offices in

Canada, at any of the yearly meetings of the said Conference in Canada, according to the Rules and Discipline of the said Wesleyan Methodist Church in Canada, which are now in force, or which may from time to time and at all times hereafter be established by the said Conference of the Wesleyan Methodist Church in Canada, with the consent and approval of the said English Conference:

NOW, THIS INDENTURE WITNESSETH, that the said Joseph Bloor, for and in consideration of the sum of Fifty Pounds, of lawful money of Canada, to him in hand paid by the said Trustees at or before the sealing and delivery of these Presents, (the receipt whereof is hereby acknowledged,) HATH given, granted, bargained, sold, assigned, released, conveyed, and confirmed, and by these presents doth give, grant, bargain, sell, assign, release, convey and confirm, unto the said Trustees by the name aforesaid, and to their successors, to be appointed as hereinafter specified, all that Parcel or Tract of Land and Premises situate, lying and being in the said village of Yorkville, in the township of York, in the county of York and Province aforesaid, containing by admeasurement eleven hundred and fifty-five superficial square yards, be the same more or less ; and which said Parcel or Tract of Land is butted and bounded, or may be otherwise known and described as follows : that is to say,—being composed of part of Lot number Twenty in the second concession from the Bay, commencing where a post has been planted on the north side of Jarvis Street, and at a distance of one hundred and thirty-two feet easterly from the East side of Yonge Street, thence North, seventy-four degrees East forty-seven feet, thence North, sixteen degrees West, seventy-one and a-half feet, then South seventy-four degrees West, forty-seven feet, then South sixteen degrees East, seventy-one and a half feet, be the said distance more or less, to the place of beginning, containing by admeasurement three thousand three hundred and sixty and a-half superficial feet, be the same more or less: Together with all and singular the buildings, messuages, tenements, hereditaments, and appurtenances whatsoever to the said Parcel or Tract of Land and Premises belonging, or in any wise appertaining, or accepted, reputed, taken, or known in part, parcel or member thereof, or of any part thereof, with their and every of their appurtenances, and the reversion or reversions, remainder and remainders, yearly and other rents, issues and profits thereof ; and all the estate, right, title, interest, inheritance, use, trust, property, possession, claim and demand whatsoever, both at law and in equity of him the said party of the first part, in, to, out of and upon, the said premises, and every part and parcel thereof, with their, and every of their appurtenances: To Have and to Hold the said parcel or Tract of Land and Premises, with all the appurtenances thereunto belonging or in any wise appertaining, TO THE USE of the said parties of the third part, and their successors in the said trust forever ; but upon the trusts, and to and for the intents and purposes, and with, and under, and subject to, the powers, provisoes, declarations, and agreements, in these presents expressed, declared, and contained, or referred to, of and concerning the same, (that is to say,)

Upon trust, that they the said parties hereto of the third part, and their successors, or the Trustees, or Trustee for the time being acting in the trusts of these presents, shall and do, with and out of the moneys now, or which may hereafter be possessed by them or him for that purpose, and as soon after the execution of these presents as conveniently may be, erect and build upon the said parcel or tract of land, or upon some part thereof, and from time to time, and at all times hereafter, whenever it shall be necessary for the due accomplishment of the trusts of these presents, or of any of them, repair, alter, enlarge, and rebuild a Church or place of Religious Worship, and a dwelling-house, or dwelling-houses, vestry-room or vestry-rooms, school-room or school-rooms, and other offices, conveniences, and appurtenances, or any of them respectively, as, and in such manner as, the Trustees for the time being of these presents, shall from time to time deem necessary or expedient:

And upon further trust, from time to time, and at all times after the erection thereof, to permit and suffer the said Church or place of Religious Worship with the appurtenances, to be used, occupied, and enjoyed, as and for a place of Religious Worship by a congregation of the Wesleyan Methodist Church in Canada in connection with the English Conference as aforesaid, and for public, and other meetings, and services, held according to the Rules and Discipline and general usage of the said Church; and do and shall from time to time and at all times hereafter, permit and suffer such person or persons as are hereinafter mentioned or designated, and such person and persons only, to preach, and expound God's holy word, and to perform the usual acts of Religious Worship therein, and Burial services in the Burying-Ground thereto belonging; that is to say, such person and persons as shall be from time to time approved, and for that purpose duly appointed, by the said Conference of the said Wesleyan Methodist Church: and all such other person or persons as shall be thereunto, from time to time duly permitted or appointed, (according to the Rules and Discipline of the said Wesleyan Methodist Church,) by the Superintendent Minister for the time being, of the Circuit in which the said Church or place of Religious Worship shall for the time being be situated; and also such other person and persons, as shall be thereunto from time to time duly appointed, by any authority lawfully constituted by the said Conference, to fill up any vacancy or vacancies, at any time occasioned by the death, removal, or suspension of a Minister or Ministers, in or during any interval between the sittings of the said Conference, but only until the then next Conference, and in no case any other person or persons whomsoever:

And upon further trust, from time to time, and at all times hereafter, to permit and suffer such Minister or Ministers of the aforesaid Wesleyan Methodist Church in Canada, to reside in, use, occupy and enjoy, free from the payment of any rent for the same, the dwelling-house, or dwelling-houses, with the appurtenances, (if any there be) erected thereon for that purpose during such time and times as the said Minister or Ministers shall and may be duly authorized so to do, by his or their being appointed by the Conference of the said Wesleyan Methodist Church in Canada, according to the Rules and Discipline thereof, to the Circuit or Station in which the same may be situated, without the let, suit, hindrance or denial of the said Trustees, or of any person or persons on their or any of their behalf:

And it is hereby declared, that, the times and manner of the various services and ordinances of Religious Worship, to be observed and performed in the said place of Religious Worship, shall be regulated according to the Rules and Discipline and general usage of the said Methodist Church: and that the officiating Minister for the time being, whether appointed by the said Conference, or permitted or appointed by the said Superintendent Minister for the time being, or otherwise permitted or appointed as in these presents is mentioned, shall have the direction and conducting of the same worship, in conformity nevertheless to the said Rules and Discipline and general usage of the said Methodist Church:

Provided always, that, no person or persons whomsoever, shall at any time hereafter, be permitted to preach or expound God's holy word, or to perform any of the usual acts of Religious Worship, upon the said parcel or tract of land and hereditaments, nor in the said Church or place of Religious Worship and premises, or any of them, or any part or parts thereof, nor in or upon the appurtenances thereto belonging, or any of them, or any part or parts thereof, who shall maintain, promulgate, or teach any Doctrine or Practice contrary to what is contained in certain Notes on the New Testament, commonly reputed to be the Notes of the said John Wesley, and in the First Four Volumes of Sermons, commonly reputed to be written and published by him:

And upon further trust, in case a School-room or School-rooms shall be erected, or provided upon the said parcel or tract of land, or any part thereof, as aforesaid, or, if there shall be no separate School-room or School-rooms, and it shall by the Trustees for the time being, of these presents, or the major part of them, be thought necessary or expedient to hold and teach a Sunday or other school or schools, in any proper part of the said Church or place of Religious Worship, then to permit and suffer a Sunday or other school or schools, to be held, conducted, and carried on from time to time, in the School-room or School-rooms, or, if it shall be thought necessary or expedient as aforesaid, in the said Church or place of Religious Worship as aforesaid, but if in the said Church or place of Religious Worship, then only at such hours and times as shall not interfere with the Public Worship of Almighty God therein : and in all places, whether in the said Church or place of Religious Worship or not, under such government, orders, and regulations as the said Conference have directed or appointed, or shall hereafter from time to time direct or appoint ; and also, subject always, to the proviso hereinbefore contained respecting doctrines :

Provided always, that, it shall be lawful for the Trustees for the time being, of these presents, or the major part of them, when and so often as they shall deem the same necessary or expedient, to take down and remove the said Church, vestry-room or vestry-rooms, school-room or school-rooms, dwelling-house or dwelling-houses, offices, conveniences, or appurtenances to the said Church or place of Religious Worship and premises belonging, or appertaining, or all, or any of them, or any part or parts thereof, respectively, for the purpose of rebuilding the said Church or place of Religious Worship, or for the purpose of building or re-building, any other vestry-room or vestry-rooms, school-room or school-rooms, dwelling-house or dwelling-houses, offices, conveniences, and appurtenances, or enlarging, or altering the same respectively, or all, or any of them, so as to render the premises better adapted to, and, for the due accomplishment of the trusts, intents, and purposes, of these presents :

And it is hereby declared, that, from time to time, and at all times hereafter, it shall and may be lawful to and for the Trustees, for the time being, of these presents, or the major part of them, to mortgage, and for that purpose to appoint, convey, and assure, in fee, or for any term, or terms of years, the said parcel, or tract of land, Church, or place of Religious Worship, hereditaments and premises, or any part or parts thereof, respectively, to any person or persons whomsoever, for securing such sum or sums of money, as may be requisite or necessary, in, or for, the due execution and accomplishment, of the trusts and purposes of these presents, or any of them, according to the true intent and meaning thereof ; Nevertheless, it is hereby declared, that, no mortgage or mortgages, nor any disposition whatsoever by way of mortgage, shall at any time hereafter be made of the said Trust premises, or any of the parts thereof, under or by virtue of these presents, unless such mortgage or mortgages, shall in the aggregate amount to, and cover the whole debt, or the aggregate amount of the whole of the debts, which at the time of the execution of such mortgage or mortgages, shall be due and owing, either legally or equitably, in respect, or on account of, or in relation to, the said Trust premises, or from the said Trustees, for the time being, or any of them, for on account, or in respect of, the said Trust Premises, or some part or parts thereof, respectively, excepting only such debt and debts, as may then be accruing, due, for, or on account of, the ordinary current expenses of the said Church or place of Religious Worship and premises; But it is hereby declared, that it shall not be incumbent upon any mortgagee or mortgagees, or upon any intended mortgagee or mortgagees, of the said Trust premises, or any part or parts thereof, to inquire into the necessity, expediency, or propriety, of any mortgages, which shall be made, or be proposed to be made, under or by virtue of these presents, or whether the same is, or are made, or intended to be made, for the whole amount of the debt, or of the aggregate amount of the debts, which shall be so due and owing as aforesaid; Nor shall anything in these presents contained, or which may be contained in any such mortgage or mortgages, extend, or be construed to extend, unless where the contrary shall, with the full knowledge and consent of the said Trustees, for the time being, or the major part of them, be therein actually expressed, to hinder, prevent, or make unlawful, the taking down, removing, enlarging, or altering, the said buildings and premises, or any of them respectively, as in these presents before mentioned and provided for, in that behalf, nor in any manner to hinder, prevent, or interfere with, the due execution of the Trusts or purposes of these presents or any of them, so long as such mortgagee or mortgagees, his, her, or their heirs, executors, administrators, and assigns, shall not be in the actual possession, as such mortgagee or mortgagees, of the hereditaments comprised, or to be comprised, in such mortgage or mortgages: anything in these presents contained to the contrary, in anywise notwithstanding:

And upon further trust, from time to time, and at all times hereafter, to let the pews and seats in the said Church or place of Religious Worship, at a reasonable rent or reasonable rents, [reserving as many free seats for the poor, where, and as may be thought necessary or expedient,] and, if there shall be any such dwelling-house or dwelling-houses, school-room or school-rooms, or other building or buildings, or any of them, erected and built as aforesaid, then to let the same, or any of them, [other than such as shall or may have been erected and built for or appropriated to the use and occupancy of the Minister or Ministers duly appointed to the Circuit or Station in which the same shall be situated,] at a reasonable rent, or reasonable rents, and also, if there shall be a cemetery or burial-ground, to let graves and tombs, at a reasonable rent or reasonable rents, or to sell graves and tombs, at a reasonable price or reasonable prices, and to collect, get in, and receive, the rents, profits, and income, to arise in any manner from the said premises, [excepting moneys which shall from time to time arise from collections and subscriptions duly made therein, according to the Rules and Discipline and general usage of the said Methodist Church, for other purposes, than for the immediate purchases of the said Trust estate,] as and when the same shall, from time to time, become due and payable, but not, [excepting as to moneys from time to time received for graves and tombs,] by way of anticipation, further than for the quarter or half-year, or year, as may be thought most expedient:

Provided always, that, when and so often as such dwelling-house or dwelling-houses as may have been erected for the express use of the Minister or Ministers of the Circuit or Station, shall not be required for the use of such Minister or Ministers on account of his or their being unmarried or otherwise, it shall and may be lawful for the said Trustees, by and with the advice and consent of the Superintendent Minister of the Circuit or Station, to let the same, and appropriate the rent arising therefrom towards paying and satisfying the board and lodging of such Minister or Ministers, or towards paying the rent for a more suitable and convenient residence or residences for such Minister or Ministers:

And it is hereby declared, that, the Trustees and Trustee, for the time being, of these presents, shall stand and be possessed of the money, arising from the said rents, profits, and income, [except as aforesaid,] upon trust, thereout to pay, in the first place, such duties, taxes, rates, and other outgoings, (if any,) as from to time shall be lawfully payable, in respect of the said premises, or any part or parts thereof : and also the costs, charges, and expenses of insuring, and keeping insured, the said trust premises, against loss or damage by fire, in such sum or sums, as the said Trustees, for the time being, or the major part of them, shall from time think proper or expedient, and in repairing and keeping the said trust premises in good repair and condition : and likewise the interest of all principal moneys borrowed, and then due and owing on security of the said trust premises, or of any part or parts thereof, by virtue of these presents ; and then, to retain to, and reimburse themselves respectively, all costs, charges, and expenses, lawfully incurred and paid by them, in or about the due execution of the trusts of these presents, or any of them ; and in the next place, thereout to pay and discharge the necessary costs, charges, and expenses, from time to time incurred, in cleansing, warming, lighting, and attending to the said Church, or place of Religious Worship, and premises ; and generally, to liquidate any debts, costs, charges, incumbrances, and expenses, at any time lawfully incurred under, or occasioned by, the due execution of the trusts of these presents, or any of them, and not included in any of the provisions aforesaid :

And upon further trust, from time to time, to pay and apply any surplus money remaining after the due payment of all such lawful debts, costs, charges, incumbrances, and expenses as aforesaid, (but according, and in conformity to the Rules and Discipline of the said Methodist Church,) for or toward the support of the Minister or Ministers, for the time being, respectively appointed by the said Conference, or otherwise, as aforesaid, either in the Circuit in which the said Chapel or place of Religious Worship, shall for the time being, be situated, or in that and some other Circuit or Circuits, or in some other Circuit or Circuits only ; or, for or towards the purpose of assisting or increasing the funds of any other Church or place of Religious Worship, or Churches or places of Religious Worship, appropriated to the use of the said Methodist Church, or in building any new Church or place of Religious Worship, or Churches or places of Religious Worship, for the use of the said Methodist Church, and which shall be settled, upon such, or similiar trusts, ends, intents, and purposes, as are in these presents mentioned ; or in subscribing, or giving to any of the general funds, objects, or charities, of the said Methodist Church : or for, or towards all, or any of the purposes, objects, funds, or charities, hereinbefore mentioned, in such manner as the Trustees, for the time being, of these presents, or the major part of them, shall, from time to time, think necessary or expedient :

And it is hereby declared, that, it shall be lawful for the Trustees, for the time being, of these presents, or the major part of them, (although there shall not then be any such surplus money as aforesaid,) from time to time, to subscribe or give, such sum or sums of money, as they shall think necessary or expedient, and may be conveniently spared, from the funds of the said Church or place of Religious Worship, for, or towards all or any of the purposes, objects, funds, or charities aforesaid :

And it is hereby declared, that it shall be lawful for the Trustees, for the time being, of these presents, or the major part of them, at any meeting to be convened and held as hereinafter mentioned, from time to time, and at all times hereafter, at their discretion, to appoint any person or persons of decent and sober conduct and good reputation, to be a Steward or Stewards of the said Church or place of Religious Worship, and at their will and pleasure to remove and to dismiss such Steward or Stewards, or any of them : and the duty of the Steward and Stewards of the said Church or place of Religious Worship, shall be, to see and attend to, the orderly conducting of the secular business and affairs of the said Church or place of Religious Worship, under the direction and superintendence of the Trustees for the time being, of these presents, or the major part of them : And also in like manner to appoint any proper person or persons, to be a Treasurer or Treasurers, of the funds of the said Church or place of Religious Worship and premises, and at their will and pleasure, to remove and to dismiss such Treasurer or Treasurers, or any of them :

And it is hereby declared, that the Trustee or Trustees, for the time being, of these presents, shall themselves, or by their Steward or Stewards, Treasurer or Treasurers, keep a Book or Books of Accounts, in which from time to time shall be plainly, legibly, and regularly entered an account of every receipt and disbursement by them, him or any of them received, or made, and also, of all debts and credits, due to, and owing from or in respect of, the said trust-premises, or any part or parts thereof, and also, of all other documents, articles, matters, and things, necessary for the due and full explanation and understanding of the same Book or Books of Accounts: and shall also in like manner, keep a Book or Books of Minutes, in which, from time to time, shall be plainly, legibly and regularly entered Minutes of all Trustee Meetings, from time to time, held under, or by virtue of these presents, and of the resolutions passed, and of all proceedings, acts, and business, had, taken, and done thereat, and also of all documents, articles, matters, and things, necessary for the due and full explanation and understanding of the same Minutes, and all other things, done in, and about the execution of the trusts of these presents; and shall and will, from time to time, and at all seasonable times hereafter, upon the request of the Superintendent Minister, for the time being, of the Circuit, in which the said Church or place of Religious Worship, shall, for the time being, be situated, produce, and show forth to him, and to every person whom he shall desire to see the same, all and every such Book or Books of Accounts and Minutes, documents, articles, matters, and things, and permit and suffer copies, or abstracts of, or extracts from them or any of them, to be made and taken, by the said Superintendent Minister, or any person or persons whom he shall, from time to time, desire to make and take the same :

And the said Book and Books of Accounts and Minutes, and all documents, articles, matters and things, relating in anywise to the said trust-premises, shall, at least once in the year, and oftener if the said Superintendent shall at any time desire, and shall give notice thereof, in manner hereinafter mentioned, be regularly, upon a day to be appointed by the said Superintendent, for the time being, or with his concurrence, examined and audited, by the Superintendent and the Circuit Steward, or Circuit Stewards, if more than one, for the time being, of the Circuit in which the said Church or place of Religious Worship shall, for the time being, be situated, at a meeting convened for that purpose: And of every such meeting Fourteen Day's Notice in writing, specifying the time, place, and purpose of such meeting, shall and may be given under the direction of the said Superintendent, for the time being, by any one or more of them, the said Trustees and Trustee, for the time being, to each and every the other and others of them, the said Trustees and Trustee, Circuit Stewards and Circuit Steward, for the time being, and either personally served upon him and them respectively, or left for, or sent by the post to, him and them, at his and their most usual place and places of abode or business :

And in order to facilitate the auditing of the said accounts, minutes, articles, matters and things, it shall be lawful for the said Superintendent, Circuit Steward and Circuit Stewards, for the time being, as aforesaid, or either or any of them, to appoint in writing a Deputy or Deputies, to act therein for them and him respectively, as aforesaid, and for that purpose, any one or more of them, may be the Deputy or Deputies, of the other or others of them, the said Superintendent, Circuit Steward and Circuit Stewards: And it is hereby declared, that the signatures of all of them, the said Auditors, Deputies and Deputy, or of the aggregate majority of them, written in the said Book and Books of Accounts and Minutes respectively, shall be sufficient evidence that all the matters and things relating to the said trust-premises, which were, up to that time, included in the said books, accounts, minutes, and documents, were duly examined, audited and approved of, unless and except so far as the contrary shall be therein by them, or by the aggregate majority of them, in writing expressed:

And it is hereby declared, that every meeting for the purpose of taking into consideration the propriety of making any alteration of, or any addition to or mortgage or sale of, the said Church or place of Religious Worship and Premises, or any part or parts thereof, or for contracting any debt, upon, for, or on account thereof, (other than for the ordinary current expenses thereof,) or for letting any such house or houses, school-room or school-rooms, as aforesaid, or for fixing the rents or prices, or making or altering rules to ascertain the rents or prices, of such graves, tombs, pews, and seats, as aforesaid, or for appropriating the funds, or any part of the funds, of the said Church or place of Religious Worship, (otherwise than for the due payment of the ordinary current expenses thereof,) or for bringing or defending any action or actions, suit or suits, respecting the said trust estates and premises, or any parts thereof, or any matter relating thereto, or for any one or more of the above purposes, shall be, and shall be deemed and taken to be, a special meeting; and of every such meeting fourteen days notice in writing, specifying the time, place, and purpose or purposes of such meeting, and signed by at least either two of the Trustees for the time being, of these presents, or by the Superintendent Minister for the time being, shall be given to the other and others, of them and him, the said Trustees, and Superintendent Minister, (unless where he is himself the person giving such notice,) and either personally served upon him and them, or left for, or sent by the post to him and them respectively, at his and their most usual place or places of abode or business:

And for the purpose of transacting their ordinary business relating to the said Church or place of Religious Worship and premises, or for any other purpose relating to these presents, or trusts thereof, (except where fourteen days notice is expressed or required as hereinbefore is mentioned,) a meeting of the Trustees for the time being, of these presents, may be held, with the said Superintendent, for the time being, as aforesaid, so soon as the same can be conveniently convened, by notice in writing, specifying the time and place of such meeting, given and signed by at least either two of the said Trustees, for the time being, or by the said Superintendent, for the time being, and either personally served upon, or left for, or sent by the post, as aforesaid, to, the other and others of them respectively, at his and their most usual place and places of abode or business:

Provided always, and it is hereby declared, that no meeting held under or by virtue of these presents, shall be invalid, or the resolutions thereof, void or impeached, by reason that any such notice or notices, as aforesaid, may not, or shall not, have reached any Trustee or Trustees, for the time being, of these presents, who, at the time of any such meeting, happens to be out of the Province, or who, or whose place or places of abode or business, shall not be known to, or cannot reasonably be found or discovered by, the person or persons who is or are respectively, as aforesaid authorized, to give any such notice or notices as aforesaid :

And it is hereby declared, that, at any meeting held under or by virtue of these presents, or of the trusts hereof, or any of them, the votes of the persons present and entitled to vote, or the votes of a majority of them, shall decide any question or matter proposed at such meeting, and respecting which such votes shall be given ; And in case the votes shall be equally divided, then the Chairman of such meeting shall give the casting vote, and which casting vote he shall have, in addition to the vote which he shall be entitled to, in his character of Trustee, Superintendent Minister, or otherwise :

And it is hereby declared, that, whenever it shall be thought necessary, or expedient to do anything in and by these presents directed, authorized, or made lawful to be done, the necessity or expediency, of doing the same shall, in like manner, be decided by the persons present, and entitled to vote upon the question to be determined, or by the majority of them, and if there shall be an even division, then by such casting vote as aforesaid : and all acts and deeds, done and executed in pursuance of any such decision as aforesaid, at any such meeting as aforesaid, shall be good, valid, and binding, on all persons entitled to vote at the meeting, who may be absent, or being present, may be in the minority, and on all other persons claiming, under or in pursuance of these presents : but no person, (unless where the contrary is hereinbefore expressly mentioned,) shall be allowed to vote in more than one capacity, at the same time, or on the same question, although holding more than one office at the same time, in the said Methodist Church, or in the same meeting :

And it is hereby declared, that the "Rules and Discipline, and General Usage," of the said Wesleyan Methodist Church in these presents mentioned or referred to, are the Rules and Discipline of the said Church, as printed and published by authority of the said Conference, in a book entitled, "The Doctrines and Discipline of the Wesleyan Methodist Church in Canada," and the General Usage and Practice of the Societies belonging to said Church, and such Rules and Regulations as may from time to time be made or adopted by the said Conference, and printed and published in their Annual Minutes, in accordance with the provisions contained in the said book of Discipline, and in the Articles of Settlement and Re-Union hereinbefore mentioned, for altering or amending the same; but subject at all times to the Proviso respecting Doctrines in these Presents contained:

Provided always, and it is hereby declared, that, excepting where the contrary is in these presents expressly declared, or provided for, the Superintendent Minister for the time being of the Circuit or station in which the said Church or place of Religious Worship shall for the time being be situated, or his Deputy thereunto from time to time by him nominated and appointed in writing under his hand, shall be chairman of, and shall preside at, and shall have a vote as such Superintendent Minister or Deputy in all meetings held under or by virtue of these presents; but in case the said Superintendent Minister for the time being, or his Deputy to be so appointed as aforesaid, shall at any time neglect to attend at any such meeting as aforesaid, or if the said Superintendent Minister or his Deputy appointed as aforesaid, shall attend, but shall refuse to act as the Chairman at any such meeting as aforesaid, or if the said Superintendent Minister shall not attend any such meeting, and shall neglect to appoint a Deputy as aforesaid, then, and in every and any of the said cases, it shall be lawful for the persons for the time being composing such meeting, and entitled to vote thereat, or for a majority of them, to elect and choose from among themselves a Chairman to preside for the time being at any such meeting as aforesaid, and every meeting so held upon any such neglect or refusal of the said Superintendent Minister or his Deputy as aforesaid, shall be as valid and effectual as if the said Superintendent or his Deputy as aforesaid had been the Chairman thereof, and had presided thereat:

Provided always, and it is hereby declared, that it shall and may be lawful to and for the Trustees for the time being of these presents, with the consent of the said Conference, such consent to be testified in writing under the hand of the President for the time being of the said Conference, at any time or times hereafter, absolutely to sell and dispose of the said parcel or tract of land, church, or place of religious worship, hereditaments and premises, or of such part or parts of the same, respecting which such consent in writing as aforesaid shall be given, either by public sale or private contract, and together, or in parcels, and either at one and the same time, or at different times, for the best price or prices, in money, that can be reasonably obtained for the same, and well and effectually to convey and assure the hereditaments and premises so sold, to the purchaser or purchasers thereof, his, her, or their heirs and assigns, or as he, she, or they shall direct or appoint; and the hereditaments and premises so sold, and conveyed, and assured as aforesaid, shall thenceforth be held and enjoyed by the purchaser or purchasers thereof, his, her, and their heirs, executors, administrators, and assigns, freed, and absolutely discharged from these presents, and from the trusts hereby declared, and every of them; and the Trustees and Trustee for the time being, acting in the trusts of these presents, shall apply the money which shall arise from every such sale as aforesaid, so far as the same money will extend, to the discharge of all the incumbrances, liabilities, and responsibilities, whether personal or otherwise, lawfully contracted or occasioned by virtue of these presents, or in the due execution of the trusts thereof, or of any of them; and subject thereto, either for or toward promoting the preaching of the Gospel in the said Methodist Church, in the Circuit or Station in which the said Church, or place of Religious Worship shall, for the time being situated, or, for the purpose of procuring a larger and more conveniently or eligibly situated parcel of tract of land, and Church or place of Religious Worship, and premises, in the place or stead of the said parcel or tract of land, Church, or place of Religious Worship, hereditaments and premises so sold or disposed of, to be settled upon the same trusts, and to and for the same ends, intents and purposes, and with, under, and subject to the same powers, provisoes, and declarations as are in and by these presents expressed and contained, or such of them as shall be then subsisting, or capable of taking effect:

Provided always, that if at any time hereafter, the income arising from the said parcel or tract of land, Church, or place of Religious Worship, hereditaments and premises, shall be inadequate to meet and discharge the interest of all moneys borrowed, and then due and owing upon, or on account of, the said trust premises, and the various current expenses attending the due execution of the trusts of these presents, and if the Trustees and Trustee for the time being of these presents, shall desire to retire and be discharged from the burden and execution of the said trusts, and, if no such proper persons as are hereinafter mentioned or described, can be found to take upon themselves the burden and execution of the said trusts with the responsibility and liability to be thereby incurred, then, in that case, it shall be lawful for the Trustees for the time being as aforesaid, or the major part of them, of their own proper authority, and without any such consent by the said Conference as aforesaid, to sell and dispose of the said parcel or tract of land, Church, or place of Religious Worship, heriditaments, and premises, or any part or parts of the same respectively, either by public sale or private contract, and either together, or in parcels, and either at one and the same time, or at different times, for the best price or prices in money, that can be reasonably obtained for the same: and well and effectually to convey and assure the hereditaments and premises so sold, with the appurtenances, to the purchaser or purchasers thereof, his, her, or their heirs and assigns, or as he, she, or they shall direct or appoint, and the hereditaments and premises so sold, and conveyed and assured, as last aforesaid, shall thenceforth be held and enjoyed by the purchaser and purchasers thereof, his, her, and their heirs, executors, administrators and assigns, freed and absolutely discharged from these presents, and the trusts thereby declared and every of them: And all the money arising from every such last-mentioned sale, shall be applied, disposed of, and appropriated, as far as the same money will extend, to the purposes and in the manner hereinbefore directed with respect to any sale made in pursuance, or in consequence, of such consent, of or by the said Conference as aforesaid; but it is hereby declared, that no sale shall be made by virtue of this present power or authority, unless the Trustees for the time being as aforesaid, or a majority of them, shall give notice in writing to the said Conference or to the President for the time being of the said Conference, on or before the first day of the then next annual meeting of the said Conference, their intention to make such sale, and the reasons for the same; nor unless the said Conference shall, for the space of six calendar months next after the said first day of their annual meeting, refuse or neglect either to give, grant, or provide the said Trustees and Trustee for the time being, with such pecuniary or other aid, assistance, and relief as shall enable them or him to bear and continue the burden of the execution of the trusts of these presents, or, (as the case may be) to find and provide other Trustees who will take upon themselves the burden of the execution of the said trusts.

And it is hereby declared, that the receipt and receipts of a majority of the Trustees for the time being, of these presents, shall, in all cases of payment made to them, or any of them, as such Trustees or Trustee as aforesaid, be a full discharge to the person or persons entitled to such receipt or receipts, his, her, and their heirs, executors, administrators, and assigns, for all mortgage-moneys, purchase-moneys, or other moneys therein respectively expressed and acknowledged to have been received, by any such Trustees or Trustee aforesaid; and in all cases, except for money paid and received in respect of any mortgage or sale of the said hereditaments and premises, or any part or parts thereof, as aforesaid, the receipt and receipts of any one or more of the Trustees for the time being of these presents, or any one or more of the Stewards or Treasurers for the time being, by the said Trustees for the time being, or the major part of them, duly authorized to sign and give receipts, shall be a full discharge to the person and persons entitled to such receipt or receipts, his, her, and their heirs, executors, administrators, and assigns for all moneys, [except as aforesaid] therein respectively expressed and acknowledged to have been received by any such Trustee, Steward, or Treasurer, as aforesaid:

And it is hereby declared, that it shall not be incumbent upon any mortgagee or mortgagees, purchaser or purchasers, of the said parcel or tract of land, Church or place of Religious Worship, hereditaments and premises, or any part or parts thereof respectively, to inquire into the necessity, expediency, or propriety of any mortgage, sale, or disposition of the said parcel or tract of land, Church or place of Religious Worship, hereditaments and premises, or of any part or parts thereof, made or proposed to be made, by the said Trustees or Trustee for the time being, or the major part of them, as aforesaid, or whether any such notice or notices as aforesaid, was or were duly given, or was or were valid, or sufficient, or whether any Steward or Stewards, Treasurer or Treasurers, was or were duly authorized to sign, and give receipts, as aforesaid : nor shall it be incumbent upon any such mortgagee or mortgagees, purchaser or purchasers, or any of them, or for any other person or persons, his, her, or their heirs, executors, administrators, or assigns, paying money to such Trustees or Trustee, or to their Steward or Stewards, Treasurer or Treasurers for the time being as aforesaid, to see to the application, or to be answerable or accountable for the loss, misapplication, or non-application, of such purchase or other money, or any part thereof, for which a receipt or receipts shall be so respectively given as aforesaid :

And it is hereby declared, that the Trustees or Trustee for the time being of these presents, shall not, nor shall any of them, their, or any of their heirs, executors, or administrators, or any of them, be chargeable or accountable for any involuntary loss suffered by him, them, or any of them, nor any or more of them for any other or others of them, nor for more money than shall come to their respective hands, nor for injury done by others to the said trust-premises, or to any part or parts thereof :

And it is hereby declared to be the true intention and meaning of this Indenture, and of the parties thereto, that the full number of the Trustees of the said Trust shall be not less than seven or more than twenty-one, and that when and so often as any one or more of the said Trustees, or of their successors in the said Trust, shall die, resign his office as Trustee, by and with the consent of a *two-thirds vote* of his co-Trustees, or withdraw from, or cease to be a member or members of the Wesleyan Methodist Church according to the Rules and Discipline of the said Church, the vacant place of the Trustee or Trustees so dying, resigning, withdrawing, or ceasing to be a member or members, of the said Church, shall be filled with a successor or successors, being a member or members of the said Church, of the full age of twenty-one years, to be nominated and appointed as follows : that is to say, to be nominated by the Wesleyan Methodist Minister having charge for the time being of the Circuit or Station in which the said hereby conveyed premises shall be situate, and thereupon appointed by the surviving or remaining Trustee or Trustees of the said Trust, or a majority of them, if he or they shall think proper to appoint the person or persons so nominated; and in case of an equal division of the votes of the Trustees present, at any meeting of the Trustees held for the purpose of such appointment, the Minister so in charge of the said Circuit or Station shall have a casting vote in such appointment ; and if it shall happpen at any time that there shall be no surviving or remaining Trustee of the said Trust, in every such case it shall and may be lawful for the Minister aforesaid to nominate, and the Quarterly Meeting of the Circuit or Station if they approve of the person so nominated, to appoint the requisite number of the Trustees of the said Trust, by the vote of the majority of the members of the said Meeting then present, and in case of an equal division of their votes, the Chairman of the said Meeting shall have the casting vote in such appointment ; and the person or persons so nominated and appointed Trustee or Trustees in either of the said modes of nomination and appointment shall be the legal successor or successors of the said above-named Trustees, and shall have in perpetual succession the same capacities, powers, rights, and duties, as are given to the above-named Trustees in and by these presents, and in and by the Acts of Parliament aforesaid :

Provided always, nevertheless, and it is hereby expressly declared, that in every such case, when the Trustees or Trustee so withdrawing, or ceasing to be a member or members of the said Methodist Church as aforesaid, shall make request for that purpose, in writing, to the surviving Trustees, they the said surviving Trustees shall and will, within six calendar months next after such request, under their hands and seal of office, [but at the costs and charges in the law of the person and persons making such request,] execute a Bond in a sufficient penalty or other obligation, to indemnify the Trustees or Trustee so withdrawing, or ceasing to be a member or members of the said Methodist Church as aforesaid, and every of them, their and every of their heirs, executors and administrators, of and from and against the payment of all and every sum and sums of money, costs, charges and expenses, which he, they or any of them, his, their, or any of his heirs, executors or administrators, either separately, or jointly, with any other Trustees or Trustee of the said trust-premises, may be bound, engaged, or liable to pay, in respect to the said parcel or tract of land, Church or place of Religious Worship and premises, or in or about the due execution of the trusts of these presents : or in place of such bond or obligation, shall procure the Trustees or Trustee so withdrawing or ceasing to be a member or members of the said Methodist Church, to be effectually released and discharged, of, and from and against the payment of all such sum or sums of money, costs, charges, and expenses, as last aforesaid, and from all liability on account or in respect thereof, or in otherwise relating thereto :

Provided always, that nothing hereinbefore contained shall be construed to prevent or disqualify any person or persons so withdrawing or ceasing to be a member or members as aforesaid, from being at any future time nominated, appointed and chosen (if then duly qualified) to be a Trustee or Trustees of the parcel or tract of land, Church or place of Religious Worship and Premises, under or by virtue of the powers or authorities in these presents contained, or either of them, for appointing a successor or successors of the Trustees of these presents :

Provided always, and it is hereby declared, that from time to time, and at all times hereafter, upon the decease of any Trustee or

Trustees for the time being of these presents, the surviving Trustees and Trustee for the time being of these presents, shall and will, within six calender months next after request for that pursose, in writing made to them or him, by the legal representative or representatives of such deceased Trustee or Trustees, (but at the costs and charges in the law of such legal representative or representatives,) respectively execute a Bond, (in a sufficient penalty), or other obligation to indemnify the legal representative or representatives of each and every deceased Trustee and Trustees, who shall make such request as aforesaid, his, her, and their lands, tenements, goods and chattels, of, from, and against, all bonds, debts, covenants, obligations, notes, judgments, claims and demands, whatsoever, which such deceased Trustee or Trustees has entered into, or become subject or liable to, on account or in respect of the said parcel or tract of land, Church or place of Religious Worship, hereditaments and premises, or otherwise on account or in respect, of the due execution of the trusts of these presents, or any of them : or, in place or stead of such Bond or other obligation of indemnity, shall and will, (at the choice and discretion of such surviving Trustees for the time being, upon such request, and at such costs and charges as last aforesaid,) cause, or procure of such legal representative or representatives as aforesaid, to be well and effectually released, or otherwise discharged, of, from and against, all and every such bond, debts, covenants, notes, judgments, claims, and demands as last aforesaid, and of and from every of them, and every part and parcel thereof respectively :

And the said Joseph Bloor hereby for himself, &c., [covenants a good title.]

And the said Sarah Bloor [bars her dower.]

REFERENCE DEED.

This Indenture, made this......day of ....one thousand eight hundred and......between............ of............of the first part; and ....wife of the party of the first part, of the second part; and .... the Trustees of the.........Congregation of the Wesleyan Methodist Church in Canada, in connexion with the English Conference, of the third part. Whereas a Religious Congregation or Society of Methodists have occasion and are desirous to take a conveyance of the Lands and Premises hereby conveyed for the purposes herein declared, concerning the same; and the said Religious Congregation or Society of Methodists, for the purpose aforesaid, has appointed the Trustees above named by the name aforesaid of the "Trustees of the.........Congregation of the Wesleyan Methodist Church in Canada, in connexion with the English Conference."

Now, this Indenture witnesseth that the said party of the first part, for and in consideration of the sum of......... to.........in hand paid by the said parties of the.........part, at or before the sealing or delivery of these presents, (the receipt whereof is hereby acknowledged) hath given, granted, bargained, sold, assigned, released, conveyed, and confirmed, and by these presents doth give, grant, bargain, sell, assign, release, convey and confirm unto the said Trustees of the............Congregation of the Wesleyan Methodist Church in Canada, in connexion with the English Conference, by that name, and to their successors, to be appointed as specified in a Deed, made and recorded as hereinafter mentioned, all that Parcel and Tract of Land and Premises situate in the......of......in the County of......... and Province aforesaid, containing by admeasurement.........be the same more or less, being composed of.........and which said Parcel and Tract of Land is butted and bounded, or may be otherwise known as follows, that is to say : ....

To have and to hold the said Parcel or Tract of Land and Premises, with the Tenements and all the appurtenances and privileges thereof and every part thereof, unto and to the use of the said Trustees, and their successors in said Trust forever. But nevertheless upon such and the same Trust, and to and for such and the same ends, uses, intents, and purposes, and with, under, and subject to such and the same powers, provisoes, declarations and agreements, and to be controlled, disposed of and managed by the like authorities, officers Trustees and persons appointed and to be appointed and acting and being in the same manner, and with the same duties, power, liabilities, and restrictions in every particular and respect as are expressed contained and declared or referred to in and by a Deed bearing date the twenty-fourth day of May, in the year of our Lord one thousand eight hundred and fifty, and made between Joseph Bloor of the Village of Yorkville, in the County of York, Gentleman, of the first part; Sarah Bloor, wife of the said party, of the first part, of the second part; and the Trustees of the Yorkville Congregation of the Wesleyan Methodist Church in Canada, of the third part, and registered in the Registery Office of the County of York, at twelve of the clock at noon of the twenty-fifth day of May, 1850, and inserted in the Book of Discipline of the said Wesleyan Methodist Church in Canada, in connexion with the English Conference, published by the Reverend Anson Green, D.D., at Toronto, in the year of Our Lord One Thousand Eight Hundred and Sixty-four, and to, for, or upon no other use, trust, intent, or purpose, or condition whatsoever : and this Indenture further witnesseth, that the said party of the second part, in consideration of the premises, and five shillings of lawful money of Canada to her by the said party of the second part, in hand well and truly paid, at or upon the sealing and delivering of these presents [the receipt whereof is hereby acknowledged] hath remised, released, and for ever relinquished and quitted claim, and by these presents doth remise, release, and for ever relinquish and quit claim, unto the said party of the third part, and their successors, all Dower, and all right and title thereto, which she, the said party of the second part, now hath, or, in the event of surviving her said husband, can or may, or could, or might hereafter in any wise, have or claim, whether at common law or otherwise howsoever of, into, or out of the said lands, tenements, and premises hereby conveyed :

And the said party of the first part doth hereby for .... heirs, executors, and administrators, Covenant, Promise, and Agree to and with the said parties of the third part and their successors in the said Trust, in manner following : that is to say, That the said party of the first part, at the time of the ensealing and delivery hereof, doth stand solely, rightfully, and lawfully seised of a good, sure, perfect, absolute, and indefeasible estate of inheritance, in fee simple, of and in the lands, tenements, hereditaments, and all and singular other the premises hereinbefore described, with their and every of their appurtenances, and of and every part and parcel thereof, without any manner of reservations, limitations, provisoes, or conditions, (other than those expressed in the original grant thereof from the crown,) or any other matter or thing to alter, charge, change, encumber, or defeat the same. And also that the said party of the first part now......in......good right, full power, and lawful and absolute authority to alien, convey, and dispose of the said lands, tenements, hereditaments and premises, and every part and parcel thereof, with the appurtenances unto the said parties of the......... part, and their successors in the said Trust, in manner and form aforesaid. And also, that it shall and may be lawful, to and for the said parties of the.........part and their successors in the said Trust, peaceably and quietly to enter into, have, hold, use, occupy, possess, and enjoy the aforesaid lands, tenements, hereditaments, and premises, hereby conveyed or intended so to be, with the appurtenances, without the let, suit, hinderance, interruption or denial of the said party of the first part.........heirs or assigns, or any other person or persons whomsoever, and that free and clear, and freely and clearly acquitted, exonerated, and discharged, of and from all arrears of taxes and assessments whatsoever, due or payable upon or in respect of the said lands, tenements, hereditaments, and premises, or any part thereof, and of and from all former conveyances, mortgages, rights, annuities, debts, judgments, executions, recognizances, and of and from all manner of other charges or encumberances whatsoever. And lastly, that the said party of the first part ....heirs and assigns, and all and every other person and persons whomsoever having, or lawfully claiming, or who shall or may have or lawfully claim any estate, right, title, interest, or trust, of, in, to, or out of the lands, tenements, hereditaments, or premises hereby conveyed as aforesaid, or intended so to be, with their appurtenances, or any part thereof, by, from, under or in trust for.. ......the said party of the first part.........heirs or assigns, shall and will, from time to time, and at all times, at the proper costs and charges in the law of the said parties of the............part, or their successors in the said Trust, make, do, suffer, and execute, or cause or procure to be made, done, suffered, and executed, all and every such further and other reasonable act and acts, deed and deeds, devices, conveyances, and assurances in the law, for the further, better and more perfectly and absolutely conveying and assuring of the said lands, tenements, hereditaments and premises, with the appurtenances unto the said parties of the......... part, and their successors in the said Trust, as by the parties of the .....part, and their successors in the said Trust, or their Counsel learned in the law, shall be lawfully and reasonably devised, advised, and required.

In witness whereof, the said parties to these presents have hereto set their hands and seals, the day and year first above written.

Toronto: Printed at the Conference Office, King Street East.

www.ingramcontent.com/pod-product-compliance
Lightning Source LLC
Chambersburg PA
CBHW021730220426
43662CB00008B/775